VISIBLE MAGIC
THE ART OF
OPTICAL
ILLUSIONS
ROBERT AUSBOURNE

STERLING
New York

STERLING
New York

An Imprint of Sterling Publishing
387 Park Avenue South
New York, NY 10016

ISBN 978-1-4027-6698-5

Library of Congress Cataloging-in-Publication Data

Ausbourne, Robert.
  Visible magic : the art of optical illusions / Robert Ausbourne.
    p. cm.
  Includes bibliographical references and index.
  ISBN 978-1-4027-6698-5
  1. Optical illusions. I. Title.
  QP495.A934 2012
  612.8'4--dc23
                    2011033601

Distributed in Canada by Sterling Publishing
c/o Canadian Manda Group, 165 Dufferin Street
Toronto, Ontario, Canada M6K 3H6
Distributed in the United Kingdom by GMC Distribution Services
Castle Place, 166 High Street, Lewes, East Sussex, England BN7 1XU
Distributed in Australia by Capricorn Link (Australia) Pty. Ltd.
P.O. Box 704, Windsor, NSW 2756, Australia

For information about custom editions, special sales, and premium and corporate purchases,
please contact Sterling Special Sales at 800-805-5489 or specialsales@sterlingpublishing.com.

Manufactured in China

2 4 6 8 10 9 7 5 3 1

www.sterlingpublishing.com

CONTENTS

THE ASSUMPTIVE MIND

The eyes are not responsible when the mind does the seeing.
—PUBLILIUS SYRUS, C. 100 BC

This is a book about illusions—specifically, *optical* illusions, an important distinction because there are illusions for all human senses: sight, smell, touch, taste, and hearing. A large chunk of our brainpower is devoted to vision. Human vision is more than a sense; it is a powerful, mysterious intellect that deserves a closer look.

Optical illusions are often associated with stage magicians, who use tricks to deceive and misdirect the visual system. Not surprisingly, they are often referred to as "illusionists." An illusion can also describe things that people think they see but don't actually see, such as monsters under the bed or flying saucers. This book will deal with a more specific definition of optical illusions. The illusions in this book are presented with nothing up our sleeves but dirty elbows; all known secrets will be revealed.

It has been said that optical illusions deceive our brains and that the mind, in turn, conspires to deceive us. This is not true. While we are quite capable of deceiving ourselves, the brain's visual system is incapable of deception. It is, however, a master of the art of *assumption*. Comprehension is powered by an assumptive brain. All that we see is ambiguous until the mind figures out what we are looking at. When you look at something, the mind quickly processes the scene against *what you know*. Have you ever heard the saying, "If it looks like a duck and quacks like a duck, it must be a duck." Well, your brain operates by that saying. So if you see a mallard,

OPPOSITE:
Design for a Tubular Triangle. Tony Azevedo, 2009.

your mind processes the scene and returns with a correct assumption: "It's a duck." The mind is hardwired to never return *two* assumptions, such as, "It's a duck and a tree," because that would be a delusion. The brain culls multiple cues into a single best assumptive guess. We may, with further thought, change our minds, but we have to start somewhere.

Optical illusions are visual trickery contrived to cajole our brains into reaching erroneous conclusions, based on erroneous visual assumptions. The more we learn about how the brain works, the easier it becomes to construct working optical illusions. For now, we can easily target obvious assumptions that the brain will almost always make.

Everything we see is an illusion. We are constantly bombarded by a barrage of them every day as we move about in a 3-D world. Consider the illustration on the opposite page, which shows an empty classroom. At first glance, you may not see any illusions, but the scene is full of them—thousands of them. To name just a few: The desks at the far end of the room appear smaller, yet we know that they are not—the apparent size difference is just an illusion. The two world globes are the standard thirteen inches (33 cm) in diameter, yet one looks bigger. The entire room looks distorted in our visual system, yet we know that the walls, ceiling, and blackboard are all rectangular. There are so many illusions in this scene that it would take a whole book to list them all. Nevertheless, our minds must process each of these illusions, even though we are not consciously aware of them.

Imagine that the classroom pictured is full of attentive students, each with a slightly different point of view of the room. Each student must build an accurate 3-D map of the space in order to interact with the rest of the class. The brain, using data received via the "Eye-way Highway," processes a million visual stumpers a second in order to construct the students' 3-D maps. If we could tap into one brain's data stream and understand it, we might hear an endless murmur, ". . . that wall is closer . . . this near the back . . . that border separates color and texture . . . those shadows are darker . . . I assume this color continues . . . the corners where the walls and ceiling meet do not really go off at odd angles; the room is perfectly square." The brain does all this on autopilot so that we can pursue more important tasks, such as paying attention to our surroundings.

OPPOSITE:
Classroom.
R. Ausbourne, 2009.

One glaring illusion in this classroom is the point where the two walls and ceiling meet in the upper right corner of the image. Two of the three lines here splay outward at different angles. The walls don't really meet at obtuse angles—it's just an illusion. Each viewer sees the room from a slightly different point of view, presenting each with a different illusion, yet they ignore this mundane illusion and accept that the room is a 3-D rectangle. Their brains, on the other hand, do not. Each viewer's brain must build a 3-D navigation map of the room, instantly calculating a solution based on reasonable assumptions, and each brain returns an accurate 3-D map of the room that is common to all viewers. A miracle! We perform millions of these unconscious illusion-resolution calculations on full automatic, each and every minute of every day.

The number of calculations the brain performs every second of every day in order to map 3-D space is staggering. And that's not all our brains do; they also take into account lightness and darkness, color, distance, shape, texture, and size. If we had to perform these calculations on a conscious level, we would freeze in place from data overload, and it would take us forever to find our way to the other side of a room. Our brains can do 3-D calculations so fast that a nimble person may dash into a room and reach the other side by twisting, dodging, and leaping objects without slowing down. Brainpower is greater than all the supercomputers in the world put together.

We perform very well in 3-D space despite these illusions because we can safely ignore most of them. When we are confronted by a deliberate optical illusion, it piques our curiosity. We begin to untangle the visual enigma by working the problem against a lifetime of catalogued memories and experiences—a very healthy exercise for the brain.

It rarely takes us long to work out a glimmer of truth: Hey, that line really isn't bent! Something is missing . . . The geometry is false. The colors aren't right. The two objects are actually the same size. . . . Even if we do not know exactly how an optical illusion works, we may realize that we are being deceived. We are an intensely curious species, so we find this exciting. Like a ride on a roller coaster, we relish the thrill because we know we are going to come out on the other side intact. Most of us thoroughly enjoy a good optical puzzle.

At some point, we reach *closure* with an illusion. We figure it out—we have become "one" with the illusion. Optical illusions can be highly social: If we see a particularly good one, we naturally want to share it—maybe to see someone else's reaction and validate our own response, or maybe just to prove that we aren't ready for a padded room yet. Maybe we share them because we are a "partaking" species. Whatever the reason, we love to accost friends or perfect strangers with illusions—*Hey, look at this!*

I have loved optical illusions all my life. Collecting them has been a passion, figuring them out is sometimes a challenge, and sharing them is icing on the cake. Drawing illusions can be difficult. If an illusion is meant to fade out, disappear, or exhibit illusory movement, it will—while the artist is working on it. I can tell you that drawing illusions is often like trying to paint a leaf while it's falling.

Optical illusions help us to understand reality. They sharpen our focus and firmly map our place within the colors and dimensions of everyday life. Just as we measure the quality of goodness against a villain in a favorite movie, we can measure the character of reality against the quirkiness of optical illusions.

MACHINERY OF THE EYE

All action is of the mind and the mirror of the mind is the face, its index the eyes.

—CICERO (106–43 BCE)

The human eyes, used in concert with an intelligent brain, give us an amazing picture of the world in full, rich, living color. This self-contained, exquisitely acute visual system is also able to differentiate a staggering range of textures, depth, and light. Each eye/brain camera system comes with a built-in film editor, interactive scene storage, a powerful software package, and a handy steady-cam function. The only moving parts are our eyes, and the whole system runs on blood, muscle, tissue, and bioelectricity.

According to Dr. Anya Hurlbert, MD, PhD, a neuroscientist at the University of Newcastle upon Tyne, "Human vision is not a sense; it is an intellect."[1] A single pair of eyes and the mind can do more visual processing than all the supercomputers in the world combined. As computer speed and bandwidth improve, we may see artificial vision improve, but for now each of us has a built-in system with two of the best all-purpose cameras in the known universe.

A system as complicated as human vision is bound to have some oddities associated with its workings. With some simple and fun experiments, it is easy to explore a few of these peculiarities.

OPPOSITE:
Eye. The human eye is an important component in a visual system that is able to differentiate a staggering range of textures, depth, and light.

BLIND SPOTS

Because our vision system is complicated, we require a large data cable to connect the eye to the brain. The connection needs to be large enough to carry a healthy blood supply and lots of neurons. This massive data cable, or optic nerve, enters each eyeball through an optic disc on the retina, which lines the inner surface of the eye. At this location—the "blind spot"—our field of vision is obscured, as the optic disc has no photoreceptors.

The missing area in each retina (optic disc) equals about 15 percent of our total view. This means 30 percent of our binocular vision is stone-blind. We are missing a good part of what we see because of blind spots, and we never notice the difference.

Why don't we see blank spots when we look around? Our brains have learned to "fill in" what we don't see by making intelligent guesses about what is missing, so they build a kind of story line about what we are seeing based on what we are thinking at the time. Essentially, some of what we see is digital fantasy. Our system's film editing is seamless, and we never even think about our blind spots or what might be missing in our field of vision.

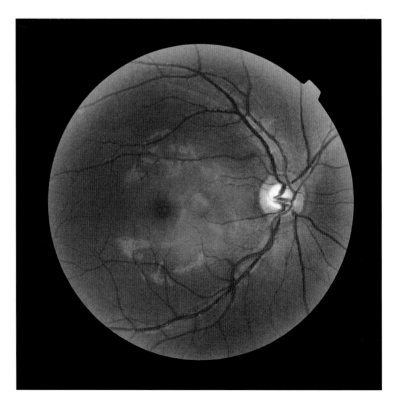

RIGHT:

The Optic Disc. The optic disc—our blind spot—is shown as a bright, yellow circle where our blood vessels and neural fibers gather to enter and exit the eyeball through the optic nerve.

Use this simple experiment to locate one of your blind spots. You won't actually see blind spots because they are invisible, but you will be able to watch a large blue circle disappear completely into a blind spot in your left eye. You will also witness the process of your mind filling in what is missing.

Close your right eye and look directly at the little eyeball at the top-right side of this figure with your left eye. Keep the blue circle in the corner of your vision, and move your head forward and backward until it completely disappears. That's your blind spot! If you wish, you can move your head side to side and up and down to get an idea of the size and shape of your blind spot. You can see it disappear and reappear as you move your head in various directions. It is not tiny, is it? Look at the color under the missing circle. Does it

match the surrounding black background color? Yes—this is the mental process of filling in. Your mind's eye has decided that you should see this color where there is none.

In the next experiment, cover your right eye and focus on the little eyeball directly to the right of the striped pattern in the figure. Move your head forward and backward to make the blue circle disappear, as you did in the first experiment. What happens to the background in this example? The mind has no problem placing the missing parts of the pattern inside the blind spot.

By the way, this green-and-yellow pattern is an illusion. The green lines are parallel, but the yellow lines are distorting them. Despite the gap in your visual field, does the illusion still work? Yes!

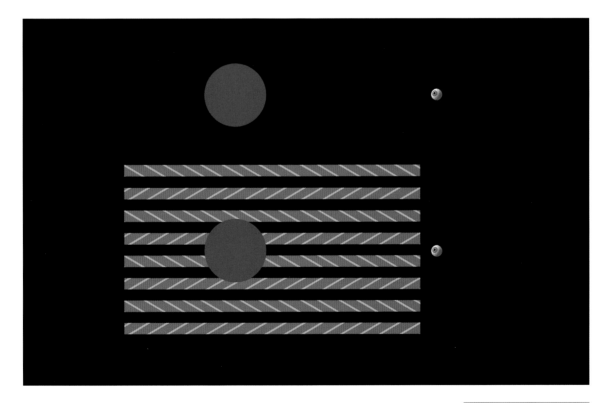

ABOVE:
Blind Spot Experiment.

VISUAL SOFTWARE

The human brain contains all the software our visual system needs to process and edit our view of the world. Visual perception begins when light waves enter the cornea and are bent into a reversed and upside-down view of the world. After arriving at the retina, the data then travels via the optic nerve to a primary processing center near the brain's center, before finally reaching the visual cortex at the back of the brain. Vision occurs at the speed of thought—which is fast, indeed.

It is a common misconception that an upright mental copy of what we see must be projected onto some kind of mental screen in the visual cortex. Not so. The brain does not rotate data, nor does it project anything. In any case, who would be inside there to see it? And yet, amazingly, you *do* see it!

Try this little exercise. Move your eyes away from this page for a moment and glance around the room. While you were looking around, many images were dancing across your retina at immense speed— several hundred feet (about 100 meters) per second. Why did you get an unbroken panorama of your surroundings instead of several jerky images? The view was contiguous because a million years of evolution has taught the mind's eye how to keep steady while you look around. The cortex gets constant updates from the eyes and knows how to synthesize them into one seamless image. With no batteries or fancy hardware, we can bounce our way through life with our own built-in steady cams!

Now, try this experiment. Close one eye and gently nudge the bottom of your open eye through the skin of the lower eyelid. Gently! Your goal is to move the eyeball ever so slightly in its socket. You will see the image rock as if there were an earthquake, even though the retina itself stays put.

ABOVE:

Fun Fact: King Charles II of England, known as the Merrie Monarch, was fond of closing one eye and then aiming the blind spot of his open eye at a prisoner's head to "decapitate" the condemned man visually before an actual beheading.[2]

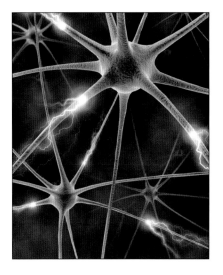

Every time you send an eye-movement signal to the brain, telling it to make your eyes "look this way" or "look that way," the brain complies with your request and sends an exact copy of the message to the visual cortex: "Hey, you are going to get an eye-movement signal. Keep the image steady!" But when you nudge the eye with a fingertip—as in this experiment—the cortex receives no "compensate for movement" response, so the image shakes. The visual cortex is wise to our every glance.

THE INFLUENCE OF EXPERIENCE

Our minds rely on innate, hardwired knowledge when perceiving an image, but individual beliefs and expectations also play a role in this process. Ambiguous images, like the one in the following figure, provide an intriguing look at the individual differences in perception.

Try this experiment. Look at the picture below. What do you see? The picture is deliberately contrived to be ambiguous. That is, it can be seen as either a young girl or as an old woman. Both aspects exist within the picture. The young woman's necklace is the old woman's thin lips, and the young woman's cheek is the old woman's nose. They share the same hat and coat.

Illusions like this one are delightful because they gently point out individual differences in perception. Some of us see one thing first; some of us the other. Scientists use terms like *top-down* or *bottom-up processing* to explain how we solve perception problems. Here's how it works: If you think about the phrase "Seven swans a-swimming," you would retrieve from memory everything you have learned about birds, colors, ponds, water, numbers, and Christmas carols in order to help build a mental image. This is called top-down processing. However, at the same time your mind's eye is processing some facts that are hardwired into your brain. This data includes things we know about surfaces, contours, depth, motion, illumination, and so on. Scientists refer to this as bottom-up processing—using what we know about the physical world to help build mental images. Our bottom-up processor works with our top-down processor to settle on a mental image to accompany the popular phrase from "The Twelve Days of Christmas."

Consider an illusion called the *Necker Cube,* a wire-frame view of a simple cube. The cube looks normal until you realize that it can be seen in two different ways—as a 3-D box with the front-most side oriented either downward or upward. It may take a moment to see both orientations, but once you recognize them, you will find that you can switch back and forth at will. You used your bottom-up processor to identify the ambiguous aspects of the cube, and you used your top-down processor to recognize it as a cube oriented at an upward or downward angle.

People with a condition known as Charles Bonnet syndrome become blind, yet they often experience hallucinations involving familiar things, such as animals and other objects. These people still have top-down processing, but their bottom-up processor, which limits delusions, lacks visual input. This seems to imply that we are delusional all the time and that normal perception is merely our bottom-up processor selecting the one delusion that most closely matches our visual input.

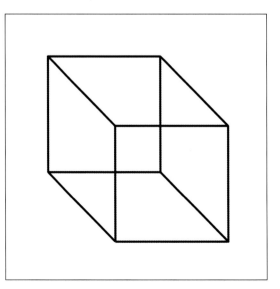

EARS OF VISION

We all know what "up" is. A lifetime of walking around in three dimensions—not to mention a few million years of evolution—has taught us this. We can usually tell if an object is tilted or not, and as long as we are upright with our feet planted on the ground, we have a pretty good handle on which way is "up," and which way is "down."

Try this simple exercise. Look around at the various objects in your room. Pick out something like a table, chair, or lamp to focus on. Now tilt your head while looking at the object. (Don't strain your neck.) It still looks upright. How does the brain know this? Remember, the master image in the cerebral cortex is not rotated, and the retinal image is upside down and reversed, anyway. The context of surrounding objects may help, but that isn't the whole answer.

What happened is that your visual cortex just got a message from your ears—specifically, the inner-ear balance gadget (the vestibular system): "We're tilting the head. Adjust for the difference." This is called *vestibular correction*. In fact, the human brain takes into account a multitude of movements that may affect our vision. However, there are limits to vestibular correction. As an example, turn this book upside down and try reading the print. For most of you, this is extremely difficult. One of the reasons may be that reading is a relatively new talent for our species—only a few thousand years have passed since the advent of writing, compared to a few million years for things like walking upright.

The next series of experiments show this perceptual reflex in action. Look at the figures below.

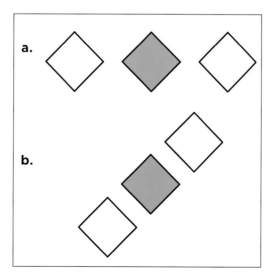

BOTTOM LEFT:
Vestibular Experiment 1. It looks like a square. Now, rotate the book 45 degrees (one-half turn) and look at the symbol. It now looks like a diamond. Rotate the book back to its normal position. Now, rotate your head 45 degrees and look at the shape. It still looks like a square!

BOTTOM RIGHT:
Vestibular Experiment 2. In this experiment, compare the set of shapes at the top of the figure to the set of shapes at the bottom of the figure. In the (a) group, the blue shape looks like a diamond. In the (b) group, however, the blue shape looks like a square. It is very tempting for us to say that our perception of the blue shape is merely being influenced by its neighbors and that there is little or no vestibular correction, but consider the next experiment.

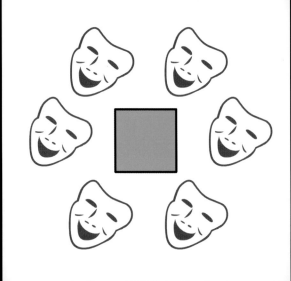

TOP RIGHT:

Vestibular Experiment 3. In this figure, we have a square surrounded by happy faces that are tilted 45 degrees. Surely, if the orientation of neighboring symbols determined how we perceived the shape in the center of the figure, we would see a diamond. And yet, it still looks as square as a square can be.

BOTTOM RIGHT:

Vestibular Experiment 4. Let's add some ambiguity to the mix. Maybe we can throw a monkey wrench into the vestibular correction process. Consider the blue shape in the image. Here, the blue shape is shown within a matrix of neighboring shapes. If you concentrate on the vertical row, the blue shape looks like a diamond. If you concentrate on the diagonal row, however, the blue shape looks like a square. It appears that context (the influence of neighboring shapes) and vestibular correction are now working hand in hand.

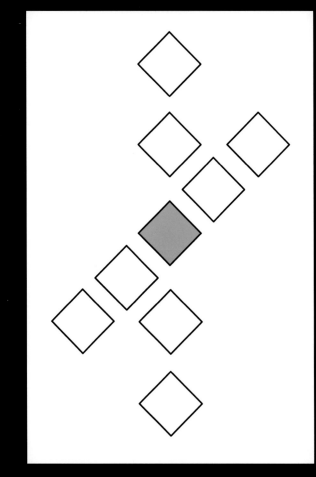

We are extremely familiar with human faces, and we have no trouble perceiving both these images as faces with our advanced spatial reasoning capabilities, even though they are upside down. We also recognize President Obama quite easily . . . but when it comes to recognizing facial expressions, we depend more on the orientation of subtle features, such as the mouth, wrinkles, eyes, and eyebrows. The mind processes facial expressions independent of the whole face—in a more advanced part of the brain. In other words, feature recognition is a more advanced mental process than facial recognition, so while our highly evolved vestibular system allows us to easily identify both images as faces, it requires more time and attention for us to notice that the features on one of the images are askew. We process the context—the face—before we process the fine details.

ABOVE:
Barack Obama.
Now, let us look at an extreme case of vestibular correction—or, perhaps, we should say non-vestibular correction. This is the *Barack Obama* illusion, a variant of the *Margaret Thatcher* illusion first developed by Peter Thompson of the University of York in England. Here, you see two upside-down images of our forty-fourth president. The images look normal, but if you turn the book around and view the images right-side up, you will see just how weird one of them is. How did we get fooled?

HOW TO TICKLE A NEURON

In 1961, two very smart Harvard neurobiologists discovered some individual neurons in the human visual system that get excited only when we are looking at certain kinds of lines.[3] Further work at Johns Hopkins University suggests that these neurons may be responding to lines that are merely *implied*. An experiment proves the existence of these little neurons.

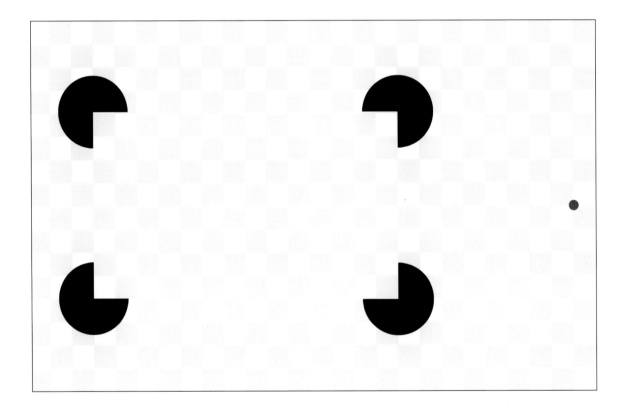

In this "subjective" illusion, pictured above, you see an image with a light checkered background. In the foreground are four black Pac-Man–like shapes. The open mouths of the Pac-Men define an illusory rectangle— let's call it a *subjective* rectangle. If the contours of this subjective rectangle are an illusion, then your target neurons must be firing as you stare at the rectangle, and their existence is thus proven. Let's further prove their existence by attempting to "tickle" the target neurons and watching their reactions.

ABOVE:
Rectangle with Illusory Contours.

Direct your attention to the small red dot to the right of the illusion. Stare at the red dot, but keep the illusion and its contours in the corner of your eye. Try not to let your eyes wander, even a little. After a few moments the illusory contours will fade away, but you will still see the bricks and the Pac-Men. What just happened?

The neurons you were using to see the contours got too "pooped to pop" as you stared at the dot. They ran out of chemical neurotransmitters and have gone off to the lunchroom to recharge, so to speak. If you move your eyes a little, new cells will become excited, and you will again see the illusion. Don't worry—you haven't harmed any cells. Tired cells soon return to work, recharged and ready to go. The neurons did, indeed, respond to our tickle.

The eight illusions on this page and the following two pages allow us to further tickle these little neurons, finding *subjective* shapes by visually tracing lines that are merely *implied*.

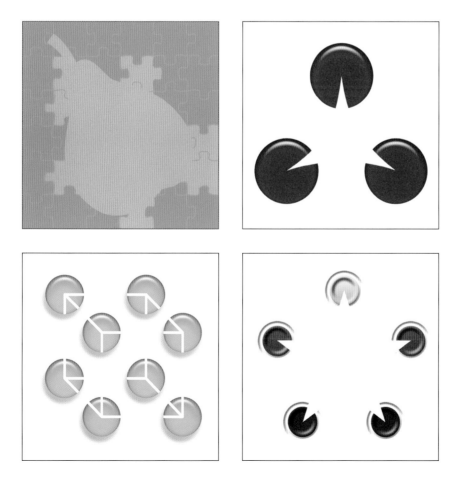

TOP LEFT:
Subjective Pear. R. Ausbourne, 2009. Can you find the outline of a plump pear in this design? It is both there . . . and not there.

TOP RIGHT:
Subjective Star. R. Ausbourne, 2009. Do you see a three-pointed star in the middle of this design?

BOTTOM LEFT:
Subjective Cube. R. Ausbourne, 2009. Can you see the outlines of a wire-frame cube design in this subjective illusion? Pronounce yourself human: We are good at making something whole out of a sum of parts.

BOTTOM RIGHT:
Color Pots and a Subjective Star. R. Ausbourne, 2009. Another subjective star defined by colored paint pots. The star seems more real than it is, but then, we're only human.

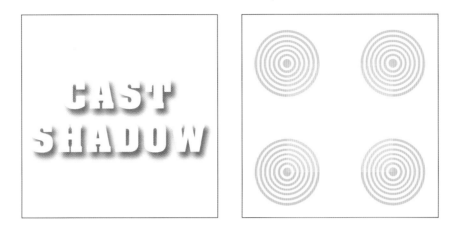

OPPOSITE:

Floating Pyramid.
R. Ausbourne, 2009.
In this scene, we see an interesting kinetic sculpture hanging over a reflective pool. Can you find a subjective floating pyramid in the scene? Look carefully at the space that the hanging shapes define with their Pac-Man–like mouths. Include the background elements in your mind's eye, and imagine this space as a floating pyramid.

TOP LEFT:

Cast Shadow.
R. Ausbourne, 2009.
The words you see here do not exist, except by virtue of the shadows being cast. If the shadows cease to exist, so do the words. Many printed words have no shadows. These shadows have words.

TOP RIGHT:

Subjective Square.
R. Ausbourne, 2009.
We see four concentric circle designs with a hint of a square showing through, yet the square is real and whole to us. Bottom-up processing: We hear and obey!

LEFT:

Mobile with Subjective Pyramid. R. Ausbourne, 2009. Can you find the subjective pyramid in this scene? It is defined by three objects in the mobile and a corner of the room.

AN UNCERTAIN UNIVERSE

Vision, in short, is controlled hallucination.

—VILAYANUR S. RAMACHANDRAN AND
DIANE ROGERS-RAMACHANDRAN[1]

Have you ever had someone tell you something and realize that it can be interpreted in a couple of different ways? When you sense that something may have more than one meaning, that is called *ambiguity*. Any and all images that find their way past our eyeballs remain *ambiguous* until our mind's eye sorts them into something that fits our personal version of reality. We all see reality from a different perspective. Ask any cop who has interviewed a crowd of witnesses: Each of us filters reality through our own perspective. Everything we see is colored by experience and blended with a generous amount of genetic information. What we believe is what we are, and what we are is what we perceive.

Ambiguous illusions—sometimes called *bi-stable figures*—are objects or scenes that are contrived to be seen in more than one way. All aspects of an ambiguous illusion share the same space. In other words, a picture must represent several potential meanings with the same set of strokes or shapes. Ambiguous figures always have at least two potential ways of being seen, but they can certainly have more than that.

There are many types of ambiguous illusions. On the following pages we explore cubes, classic allegories, figure/ground illusions, the ubiquity of faces, and other puzzles that challenge the certainty of perceptual experiences.

OPPOSITE:

The Missing Corner Cube. R. Ausbourne, 2008. This cube is three-times ambiguous. It can be seen as a normal cube that's missing a corner; as a hollow, three-sided room with a small cube sitting in the far corner; or as a small cube floating in front of a larger cube. After you see all three versions of this image, you can flip between them quite easily. Make a model of this cube, and you will find that you can still see all three versions if you hold the model in the same orientation as shown here. Rotate the model, and you will see the small floating cube in front of the large cube turn in the wrong direction!

AMBIGUOUS FIGURES

The mind silently abhors ambiguity, so we often see objects at first as what they are. As we stare at the object for a little while, however, we might see something else. If we know that an image is intended to be ambiguous from the start, we are thrilled when we discern an alternate meaning or resemblance, in the same way we suddenly *get* a joke or a puzzle we are working on.

TOP LEFT:
Mother, Father and Daughter. G.H. Fisher, 1968. There are three faces in this illusion: a young woman, an older woman, and an older man.

TOP CENTER:
Do You See A Cartoon Face or A Mouse? Anonymous.

TOP RIGHT:
A Grizzly Old Geezer or a Young Cowboy? Anonymous.

CENTER LEFT:
Rabbit or Duck? Anonymous. In this classic illusion, do you see a rabbit facing right, or do you see a duck facing left?

CENTER RIGHT:
A Harbor Seal or a Donkey? Anonymous.

BOTTOM:
Love and Hate. Josh Sommers, 2008. Two words with opposite meanings sharing the same space.

TOP LEFT:
A Face Full of People, or Several People Making a Face? Anonymous.

TOP RIGHT:
Five Clowns. R. Rusty Rust, 2008. You may see only four until you look more closely.

BOTTOM LEFT:
Woman of the World. R. Ausbourne, 2011. This globe has some familiar-looking continents. Can you find a profile of a woman in the design?

BOTTOM RIGHT:
A Falcon or a Wizard? R. Ausbourne, 2011. This design for a scary mask can be seen as a bearded wizard character or a stylized falcon.

AMBIGUOUS CUBES

RIGHT:

Three Dice or Four?
R. Ausbourne, 2008.
At first glance, this
figure looks like three
dice. Look more closely,
however. The space in
the center of the cluster
looks like . . . an empty
space. Try to imagine
that the sides of the
space do not descend
but rather protrude,
forming a fourth cube.
The fourth die is an
illusion because it
can pop in and out of
existence.

ABOVE LEFT:

*Missing Corner Cube,
Wooden Variant.* Tony
Azevedo, 2006. This
version of the *Missing
Corner Cube* illusion
may make it easier to
visualize all three illusory
aspects.

ABOVE RIGHT:

Cube Assembly. In this
cube assembly, the
geometry can change
instantly from 3-D to
hollow.

LEFT:
Baby Blocks.
R. Ausbourne, 2010.
Can you find the fourth
"subjective" toy block
in this figure? Hint: The
hidden block has no
letters on it.

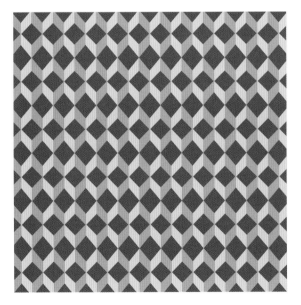

ABOVE LEFT:
A Stack of Ambiguous Cubes. These cubes all have dark-colored tops. Visualize all the cubes with dark-colored bottoms. They have now become bi-stable cubes.

ABOVE RIGHT:
Another Stack of Ambiguity. These rectangular bricks have dark faces oriented downward. Visualize all the bricks with the dark faces on top, oriented toward the upper left-hand corner. You are now in the ambiguity vortex.

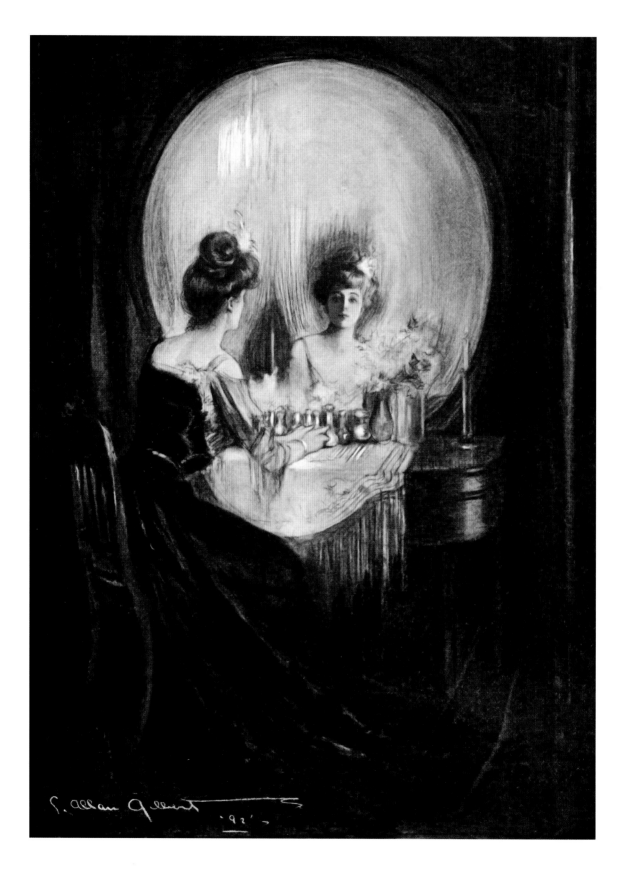

VANITAS VANITATUM, OMNIA VANITAS

The Latin *Vanitas vanitatum, omnia vanitas* translates into English as "Vanity of vanities; all is vanity." This famous quote is from Ecclesiastes 1:2, in which King Solomon expounds on the vanities of the world. The line has inspired many literary and artistic interpretations. Perhaps the most famous image associated with the quote is the allegorically ambiguous drawing by American illustrator Charles Allan Gilbert titled *All Is Vanity*. Gilbert's famous illusion, completed in 1892, can be seen as a pretty girl plus her reflection in a vanity mirror, or as an ominous skull. Both scenes in this illusion share the same pictorial elements.

The delightful rendering first appeared commercially in 1902, when it was sold and published in a small five-cent railway pamphlet. In spite of this inauspicious beginning, the drawing was a commercial hit and has since become possibly the most reproduced illusion in history. Even Rebekah Baines Johnson, teacher and mother of the thirty-sixth U.S. president, Lyndon B. Johnson, often referred to the print in her Texas classroom lectures.

Charles Gilbert is credited with many artistic achievements, including several covers for the *Saturday Evening Post*. However, artists like J. C. Leyendecker, Norman Rockwell, and, later, Andrew Wyeth captured most of the limelight. Gilbert spent much of his career in obscurity. He died in 1929 having never created another optical illusion.

OTHER CLASSIC ALLEGORIES

Popular illusions, such as *All Is Vanity*, have inspired a variety of allegorical ambiguities. The nineteenth century was a time of modesty and moral fortitude. Horatio Alger novels, with their rags-to-riches themes, were wildly popular, and the concept of "manifest destiny" imbued many Americans with a sense of divine purpose and privilege. In Victorian America, it was even common to cover piano legs with skirts. But the times were changing: The spirit of the Roaring Twenties, with its "licentious" jazz music and sexually uninhibited flappers, was already bubbling under the surface. The following images are examples of ambiguous illusions that were created during this period of changing societal norms.

OPPOSITE:
All Is Vanity. Charles Allan Gilbert, 1892. Perhaps the most reproduced optical illusion in history.

TOP LEFT:
Two Lovers or a Skull?
Anonymous.

TOP CENTER:
*L'Amour de Pierrot (A
Clown's Love).* French
postcard, c. 1905.

TOP RIGHT:
*Yesterday, Today, and
Tomorrow.* Anonymous.

BOTTOM:
Society: A Portrait.
George Wotherspoon.
A nineteenth-century
allegorical illusion by
Wotherspoon, this
image can be seen as a
dapper gentleman out
on the town. If you look
more closely, however,
you will see a donkey
head composed of the
man's torso and the
accompanying ladies'
hats. In the 1890s
(the "Gay Nineties"),
allegorical or culturally
themed illusions were all
the rage.

The Old Gypsy,
Anonymous, c. 1865.
This girl's hair reflects
the fragile nature of
beauty.

*Gossip, and Satan
Came Also.* George
Wotherspoon. Another
allegorical illusion by
Wotherspoon can
be seen as two lady
gossipers, but look
more closely, and you
will see the devil lurking
in the background. This
print is often seen as
a companion to *All Is
Vanity* and has been
erroneously accredited
to Charles Gilbert.
Wotherspoon was a
contemporary and
may have influenced
Gilbert's work.

REVERSALS

TOP:
The Long Trail.
R. Ausbourne, 2011.
Is this horse and rider
coming or going?

BOTTOM:
Mach Figure.
R. Ausbourne, 2008. A
famous reversal named
for its originator, Ernst
Mach. The book might
be open and facing you,
or it might be open and
facing away from you.
Both views are possible.
Make this illusion
yourself. Fold a piece
of paper in half, open it
up, and view it from the
angle shown. Instant
handheld ambiguity!

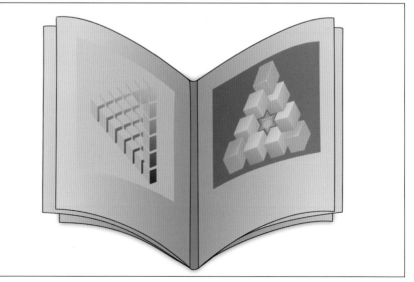

FIGURE/GROUND ILLUSIONS

Scientists often refer to the mental process of perceiving ambiguous figures as *figure/ground reversal*. There is a minuscule gap of time in our thinking process that precludes us from seeing two things at once. Most of us do not notice the time gap and often mistakenly think that we see both versions of the scene at the same time. The candle design exemplifies a classic illusion of ambiguity.

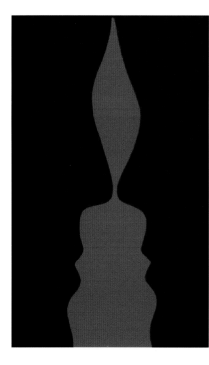

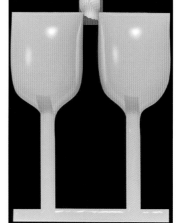

TOP LEFT:
Candle or Lovers? Anonymous. You see a drawing of either a red candle or the profiles of two lovers, face-to-face. This implies that the profiles are part of the background, and the candle is in the foreground.

TOP RIGHT:
The Loving Cup. Anonymous. A handmade leather postcard from 1864 showing a crude version of the ambiguous cup and profiles.

BOTTOM LEFT:
A Striped Goblet with Profiles. Anonymous.

BOTTOM RIGHT:
Wine and Dine. R. Ausbourne, 2011. Does this ambiguous design show one bottle, two wineglasses, or all three?

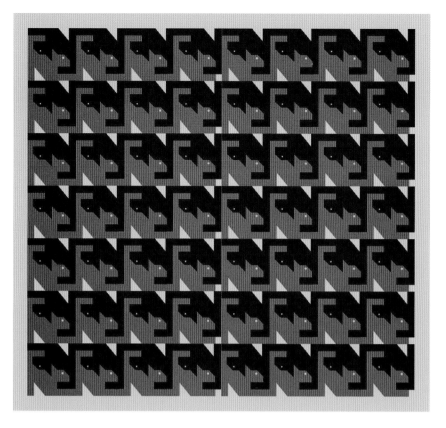

TOP:
The Eye Loves Ambiguity in Patterns.
R. Ausbourne, 2010.
Most of us will see the red cats first because they are upright. Looking closer, we notice the red-black symmetry and see black cats in a complementary, upside down position.

BOTTOM:
Don't Be Fooled.
Josh Sommers, 2008.
The spaces between these columns do double duty as silhouettes of the artist.

A WORLD OF FACES

Nature offers us ambiguity at every turn, especially in terms of objects we are very familiar with, such as faces. The first thing a baby recognizes is a human face, and for the rest of our lives we are drawn to faces. We see them in clouds, in wallpaper patterns, in leafy patterns, on peach pits, on barn doors, rock formations, even on the moon. The following images display some of my favorite examples of how human faces show up in odd places.

TOP:
Ambiguous Face on a Natural Rock Formation, Mars. Taken from NASA's *Viking I* orbiter, 1976.

BOTTOM:
Face Rock, near Bandon, Oregon. A giant's face gazes serenely heavenward, despite foul weather.

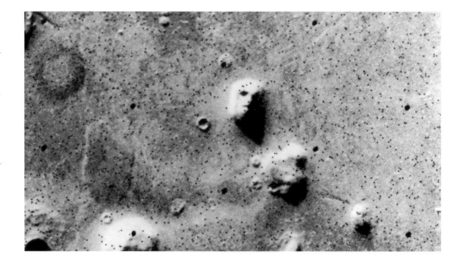

TOP:
A Happy Home.

CENTER:
Serious Little Faces.
A sprig of stern-looking
mountain spring flowers.

BOTTOM:
Landscape Head.
Wenzel Hollar,
c. seventeenth century.
If you can't find a natural
face, just make one.

HIDDEN FIGURE PUZZLES

The puzzles on the next four pages test your attention to detail and your object-recognition abilities. Some of them are new, some old, and some really ancient. (Answers for the puzzles on this page can be found on page 149.)

(Answers for the puzzles on this page can be found on page 149.)

TOP LEFT:
Puzzle 1. R. Ausbourne, 2008. Many of the pictorial elements that help distinguish foreground from background have been eliminated from this sketch. Can you tell what it is?

TOP RIGHT:
Puzzle 2. R. Ausbourne, 2007. This is another picture with skimpy visual clues. What is it?

BOTTOM:
Toll Gate No. 3. E. C. Abbey. This picture is from a c. 1888 puzzle card. There are many hidden animals and figures in this drawing. How many can you find?

TOP:
Ten Friends. R. Rusty Rust, 2007. Despite the name of this piece, there are only nine people visible. Can you identify the tenth friend?

BOTTOM LEFT:
Bonaparte Violets. **Anonymous.** This picture of a sprig of violets contains the profiles of Napoleon Bonaparte and his family. Can you find them all? When Napoleon was exiled to Elba, his followers continued to support him in secret. They used the code name "Capt Violet" and distributed many secret messages to fellow loyalists.

BOTTOM RIGHT:
Dreams. R. Rusty Rust, 2007. What is the boy dreaming about?

OPPOSITE:
Lion Country. R. Rusty Rust, 2007. A lovely African woman and her child are haloed by golden grass in this painting. Where is the lion?

TOP:
The Hidden Tiger. R. Rusty Rust, 2007. This is one of Rusty's most ingenious ambiguities. Can you figure out why? Examine the tiger very carefully.

LEFT:
Hidden Lion. R. Rusty Rust, 2007. Despite its name, this painting depicts a herd of zebra. Can you find the lion?

COLOR ON THE MIND

Think of color, pitch, loudness, heaviness, and hotness.
Each is the topic of a branch of physics.
—FRENCH MATHEMATICIAN BENOIT MANDELBROT

It has been said that color perception is merely icing on the cake, that the ability to see color is a freebie—we don't really need it to function in the world. After all, many animals do not see in color, and they do just fine. Spot, the dog, sees very little color, and he is the epitome of happiness.

Of course, try telling that to an artist like Claude Monet: "Color is my day-long obsession, joy and torment." Monet may have been comforted by recent research that suggests that seeing color is an essential part of being human.[1] All creatures see adequately, according to a need. Frogs don't see much of anything at all, unless it is moving. Eagles can see much farther than we do, and even a bunny rabbit exceeds our ability to sense the slightest movement. Many creatures can see in color but have only two color-sensing cones on their retinas. With three cones and almost half our brains devoted to the sense of sight, humans have an extraordinary ability to discern different shades of color.

Consider the full-page illustration, *Kaleidoscope,* by digital artist C. H. Brittenham. The left half is shown in full color, while the right half appears in shades of gray. The full-color half of the picture displays variety, while the other half lacks detail. An object's color depends on which wavelengths of light are reflected from the object. From this perspective, a daffodil appears yellow to us because it absorbs all colors except yellow. While this is true, it is not the whole story. Color perception involves a

OPPOSITE:
Kaleidoscope Pollen.
Chuck Brittenham, 2008. The stark contrast between the two halves of this digital rendering demonstrates the difference between seeing in shades of gray and a colorful, vibrant perception of the world around us.

top-down mental process as well. If color were merely perceived as the sum of an illuminant wavelength and a surface reflectance wavelength, the daffodil's color would change radically as the environment around it changed. For example, if only bottom-up processes were involved in the perception of color—if the color of an object depended solely on the light rays entering the eye—the color of a daffodil in deep shadow would look drastically different from the hues of a daffodil in sunlight. However, thanks to a mysterious mental phenomenon, known as *color constancy*, the color of the shaded daffodil appears as a darker shade of the same yellow. Our minds are able to hold fast to the daffodil's reflectance properties despite a wide range of changes in ambient shadow and light.

There is good news and bad news about color perception. The bad news is that we don't know exactly how it works (yet). The good news is that much of what we do know is based on research using optical illusions!

THE WATERCOLOR EFFECT

BELOW:

Watercolor Effect.
R. Ausbourne, 2009. Squares without a watercolor effect in this stained-glass illusion are easy to spot: They are completely white. Other squares with color borders seem to be tinged with a light version of the border color. Color spreads into open white areas freely, but not across solid, dark borders.

One of the things scientists are looking at closely these days is how we perceive the edges and borders of things. This may seem trivial, but it is essential to our ability to make sense of everyday objects. The brain loves borders because they help us define the extent and shape of an object and because a color usually stops at a border. Our mind is always asking itself questions like these: "Where does this color stop?" "And where does the next color begin?" Without answers, we would be left with an indistinct yellow blob instead of a delightfully detailed daffodil. The following examples show how specialized neurons may help our brain answer these questions. A recently discovered phenomenon known as the *Watercolor Illusion*[2], sometimes called *color bleeding* or *spreading*, sheds light on how we use borders to aid perception.

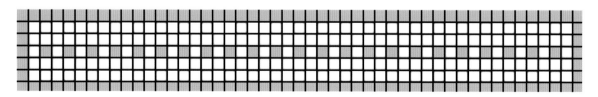

Consider the two maps shown below.[3] This is old Captain Flint's secret treasure map (missing a large red X indicating "bulk of treasure here," but that's another story). *Map 1* shows a blue band of color inside a squiggly orange border. Notice that an illusory light-blue color seems to leak or spread inward from the blue band and cover the entire island. Our minds are willing to let the blue color leak into the open areas but not over the solid orange borders. Some of our brain cells must be acting as border control agents for color perception.

Map 2 is shown with the blue band outside the island's solid orange border. In this map, the solid orange border stops the blue color from leaking into the island. In fact, old Flint's island now appears a brighter white in contrast to the white background, almost floating above the page. The blue color appears to spread outward from the solid border, giving the illusion of contour to the island and its surrounds. Thus, "border-control neurons" may be key to our understanding of how we perceive three dimensions.

BELOW LEFT:
Treasure Island Watercolor Effect: Map 1. R. Ausbourne, 2009. The light-blue color covering the island—which actually looks more like a body of water, in this case—is an illusion; only the thin blue band and solid border are real.

BELOW RIGHT:
Treasure Island Watercolor Effect: Map 2. R. Ausbourne, 2009. The watercolor illusion persists, this time spreading light-blue color outward into the "open sea" (white background).

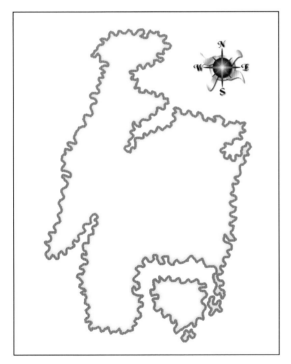

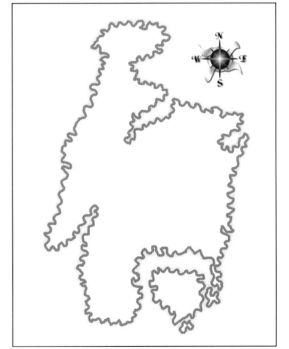

Let's look at an example that demonstrates why a solid border isn't always needed to halt the perception of contour. *Bleeding without Borders* looks very much like a sheet of purple paper that has been folded in half and then unfolded and flattened out. Of course, it really isn't paper, nor has it been folded. Rather, a very thin *shadow line* down the center of the image helps create the 3-D effect, as revealed in the colorless section at the bottom of the image. In this image, the darkness is illusory. Amazingly, without a solid border, the shading does not spread even one pixel to the left. Somehow our minds have decided that a thin shadow equals a solid border.

ABOVE:

Bleeding without Borders. R. Ausbourne, 2009. Even though it is just a thin shadow line, its influence spreads all the way to the right—the entire right half of the image appears darker. In reality, it isn't.

RIGHT:

Pinstripes.
R. Ausbourne, 2007. The blue color is the same shade throughout this illusion. The placement of black lines in the central square causes the blue in that area to appear darker than the surrounding blue.

OPPOSITE:

Plagued by Contrast.
R. Ausbourne, 2009. There are only four colors in this design. Any extra color shades that you see are purely illusory. Each color is repeated with different amounts of black nearby, which accounts for the illusory shades of color.

BATTLING COLORS

We humans are capable of discerning about 250,000 different colors. Every color we can see has an effect, to some degree, on every other color we see. When a color appears lighter or darker than a nearby color, we call the difference *contrast*.

Illusions do not prompt us to compare things—comparing is almost as natural as breathing. When we look at a figure, we immediately begin comparing it to its surroundings. This next contrast illusion example is shown in the gray scale. In the *Gray Scale* illusion, we see a long, thin band increasing from a light gray to a dark gray along its length within a band that appears to fade in the opposite direction. In fact, the thin band is one even shade of gray, end to end. You can easily prove this by covering the thick gray scale with strips of paper, leaving only the thin band exposed. The truth is that light colors make nearby colors look darker, and dark colors make nearby colors look lighter.

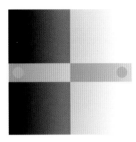

ABOVE:
Ilusory Difference.
R. Ausbourne, 2009.
The orange circles are exactly the same color and value.

TOP:
Gray Scale.
R. Ausbourne, 2009.
This illusion demonstrates how context influences our perception of color. At every point along the gray band, we cannot help but compare its uniform color with the surrounding gray scale.

BOTTOM:
The 10 Percent Solution.
R. Ausbourne, 2007.
Each block is 10 percent darker than the block before it, and, this time, the thin solid gray bar appears to darken from left to right.

The 10 Percent Solution illusion is the same illusion, except that the gray tones proceed in discrete increments from white to black. Whether or not the surrounding gray scale is discrete or continuous, the gray tone in the middle appears lighter next to darker shades and darker next to lighter shades. Over the middle, the shades of gray match.

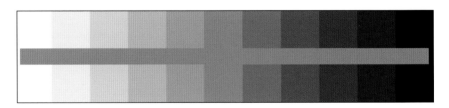

ILLUSORY SHADOWS

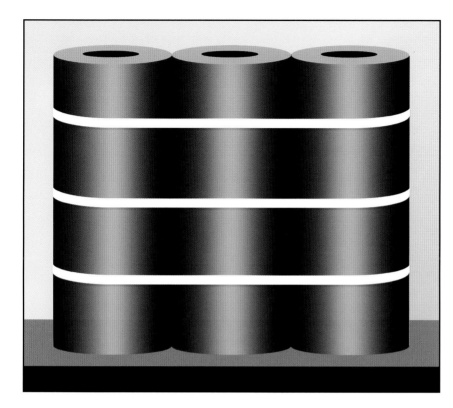

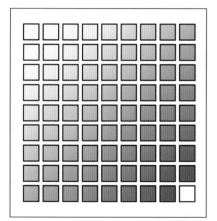

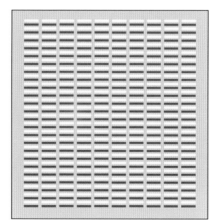

TOP:
Industrial Contrast.
R. Ausbourne, 2009.
The tape that holds these rolls of factory cargo together appears lighter when passing areas of high color contrast and darker in areas of low color contrast.

BOTTOM LEFT:
Illusory Pink Dots.
R. Ausbourne, 2008.
Do you see fuzzy pink dots in the intersections between the squares in this design? Do they appear where you are not looking? The dots fade away if you look directly at them and are less distinct in the areas with light-colored squares.

BOTTOM RIGHT:
Patterns of Contrast.
R. Ausbourne, 2009.
This design forces the eye to see extra shades of the background color. Look between the columns of alternating red and white bars, where fuzzy shadows are lurking. They will fade away if you look right at them.

THE EHRENSTEIN FIGURE EVOLVES

German psychologist Walter Ehrenstein Sr. developed a simple illusion of contrast in 1941 to demonstrate that radiated lines can often generate a bright, illusory shape in a central patch. His original design is shown below. It is clear that the center of the left-hand patch appears brighter than the one with a border.

Recent studies using the Ehrenstein figure are shedding new light on the machinery of contrast and color in the human mind.[4] In the following examples, I demonstrate five illusions using an enhanced version of the Ehrenstein figure.

RIGHT:

Ehrenstein's Figure. Walter Ehrenstein, 1941. A bright illusory patch appears in the center of a series of radiated lines around an imaginary circle. Introducing a border around the circle destroys the illusion.

TOP:

The New Ehrenstein Figure. c. 2008. More radiated lines enhance the effect.

BOTTOM:

Ehrenstein Figures with Light-Colored Borders. The bright patch is destroyed with a solid black border around the circle, but if one places a light-colored border around the circle, it actually enhances the brightness of the central patch. This discovery surprised scientists so much that they gave the phenomenon a three-word name: *anomalous brightness induction.*

The Ehrenstein figure is easy to make and fun to experiment with. Try creating some variations on your own. You may discover a brand-new illusion!

TOP:
Shimmering Ehrenstein Figures. In this experiment, a gray disk added to the central patch of the Ehrenstein figure begins to emit a shimmering effect as the eye pans over it. This effect may be attributed to a competition within the brain between the brightness illusion and the real, physical color of the gray disk.

CENTER:
The Ehrenstein Maelstrom. The whole foundation of the illusion is shaken up with a simple change: The background becomes black, and a light border appears inside the radiating lines. The power of contrast now reverses itself with a vengeance, as the bright patch now appears to be blacker than the surrounding black.

BOTTOM:
Ehrenstein Flashing Blue. This final variation of the illusion shows a gray disk surrounded by a yellow border. Here we get the effect of a shimmering gray disk with a hint of afterimage, or assimilation. The central patch appears to shimmer and seems to be tinted with the complementary color of the border's color (in this case, dark blue).

ANOTHER BRIGHT PATCH

The *Burning Fuse* illusion displays the same illusory brightness effect as found in the Ehrenstein variations we have looked at, but this illusion reveals an additional wrinkle. Thick bands that fade toward the center of the figure replace thin spokes. You may notice a very faint shadow lurking around the bright patch in the center of the cross and pinwheel shapes below.

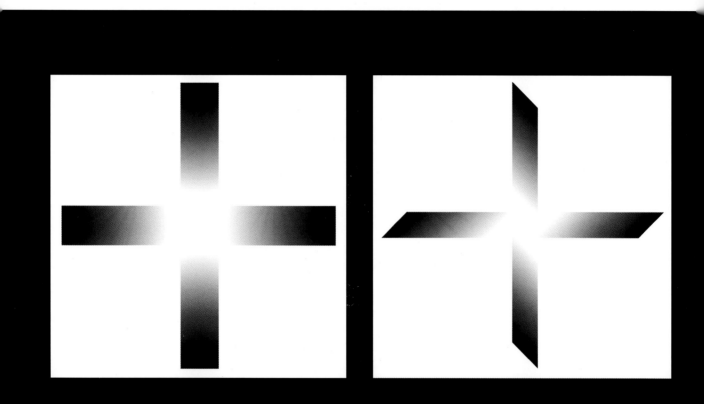

ABOVE LEFT:
Burning Fuse.
Tony Azevedo, 2009.
This figure is so bright that it looks like hot metal near the center—hence the name, "burning fuse."

ABOVE RIGHT:
Slanted Burning Fuse. Tony Azevedo, 2009. The fading dark bars define a central pinwheel of brightness. The brightness is an illusion, as is the dark halo surrounding it.

THE STROOP COLOR TESTS

American psychologist John Ridley Stroop invented three simple tests in 1935 to test our ability to read the words for various colors against our ability to identify those colors in which the words appear. Our ancestors have been identifying colors for many thousands of years. However, our ability to read printed words occurred much later in our history and uses different parts of the brain. These simple tests can show how these two abilities, pitted against each other, can sometimes make the mind stumble. Below is a key that shows the six colors and color names used in the tests.

RED   ORANGE   YELLOW

GREEN   BLUE   PURPLE

The three Stroop color tests shown on the following pages are fairly simple. The first test will establish your ability to identify the various colors, and the second test will assess your ability to read the names of various colors. These first two tests will get you ready for the last test, which is a mix of the first two. The results may surprise you. Each page contains instructions; follow them as best you can. You may even want to time yourself during these tests.

ABOVE:
Stroop Color Key.
R. Ausbourne, 2009.
The colors used in the
Stroop tests.

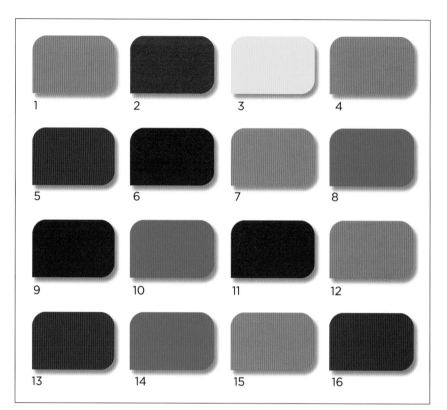

ABOVE:

Stroop Color Test 1. R. Ausbourne, 2009. This is a simple color identification test using sixteen color swatches selected at random. Start at swatch number 1 and proceed from left to right before moving on to the next row of swatches. Identify (out loud) the color of each swatch.

RIGHT:

Stroop Color Test 2. R. Ausbourne, 2009. This is a simple reading test using sixteen color names selected at random. Start at number 1 and read aloud the names for each color as you proceed, until you reach number 16. To make it extra easy, each color name exhibits the corresponding color for that word.

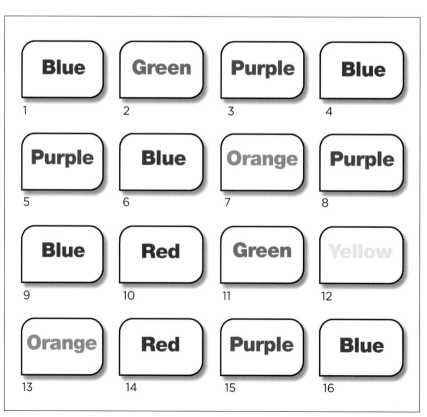

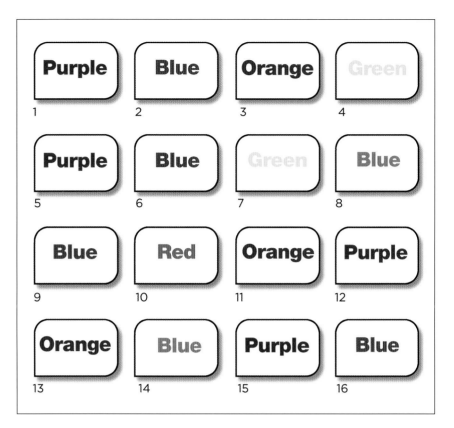

Purple 1	**Blue** 2	**Orange** 3	Green 4
Purple 5	**Blue** 6	Green 7	Blue 8
Blue 9	Red 10	**Orange** 11	**Purple** 12
Orange 13	Blue 14	**Purple** 15	Blue 16

LEFT:

Stroop Color Test 3. R. Ausbourne, 2009. This test is a mix of the last two tests . . . with a sneaky twist. The color names do not match the actual colors of the words—ignore the names! Rather, identify out loud the actual color of each word, starting with number 1. No penalties; do the best you can.

HOW TO GRADE YOUR TEST RESULTS

If you are like the rest of us mere mortals, you will not do as well with the last Stroop color test. Our brains are likely to stumble over the identification of the colors as we go through the test because we are tempted to read the words. In some cases, we blurt out the word first and then go back and identify the correct color, so it usually takes a bit longer to complete the last test as we fumble through the answers. Rest assured: You are normal. We use one part of our brain to read printed words and another area to identify colors, so being forced to juggle these two mental abilities can be a mind-expanding exercise. Try giving the tests to your friends—it is reassuring to watch them muff up the last test.

4
ONE-HALF TWIST
FROM REAL

Impossible objects are reasonable parts put together in unreasonable ways.

—ROBERT AUSBOURNE

An "impossible object" is a little wrinkle in the fabric of normalcy. At first it appears familiar to us, but then we perceive that something is askew. We pause to sort out the problem, as if it were a child with his buttons done wrong. Individual parts of the object look normal, but, on the whole, the geometry is wrong. It is almost as if someone had taken a normal object and wrenched it around one-half twist. Take a look at digital artist Josh Sommers's rendering of a precision balancing mechanism (shown below), and you sense that something is wrong. Not only is this amazing structure incapable of doing useful work, it cannot exist. The balance arm cannot intersect with both upright segments at the same time—not in this universe, anyway. It's an impossible object.

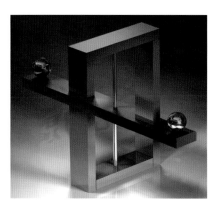

You can draw impossible objects, but you can't build them because they are outside the laws of nature. All drawings of impossible objects are designed to be viewed from one special point in space called the *Ames transformation*. The Ames transformation is the one point of view from which the

LEFT:
Impossible Balance.
Josh Sommers, 2009.

OPPOSITE:
Stones Unhenged.
R. Ausbourne, 2005.

object looks impossible. From all other viewing angles, the object looks normal and "possible."

Compare two views of a rendered object (a) and (b) in the following figure. Object (a) is seen from its Ames transformation point of view and appears impossible. In view (b), the same object is shown rotated away from its Ames transformation point of view. Now it looks boring, ordinary, and very possible.

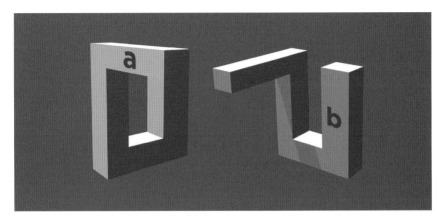

It is feasible to build a 3-D model that mimics an impossible object, but you would have to present the model from its Ames transformation angle. You could stand next to the model and tell viewers, "Look at it from over here," or you can photograph the model from that viewpoint and present it in print . . . in which case you are right back in flat, 2-D land. Another way to present an impossible model is to put it into a box with a single peephole in the right position. A box for this purpose is called an *Ames room*."

Personally, I think it is easier to use a 3-D drawing program on a computer to create impossible objects. Since they are flat and frozen in time, images of impossible objects represent a sort of 2-D Ames room: Viewers are always looking at the model from an imaginary peephole at the perfect angle.

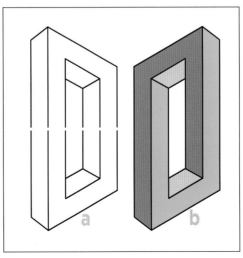

OPPOSITE:
Bent Square.
R. Ausbourne, 2005.
The square on the table looks bent because of the two support columns. However, the square isn't really bent, and the columns are somewhat less than they seem. The scene was rendered normally; the columns were altered in postproduction.

TOP:
Ames Transformation–Comparison.
R. Ausbourne, 2007.

BOTTOM:
Make an Impossible Square Design.
R. Ausbourne, 2010.
Start with a 3-D trapezoidal border tipped on its side, with equally spaced vertical lines. Cut it in half, as shown in (a). Reverse the top half of the figure so that it is facing the opposite direction, and put the two halves back together (b). The object now has the magic half-twist.

OPPOSITE:
Remote Phone.
R. Ausbourne, 2008.
If you happen to be in
Roswell, New Mexico,
and see this public
phone booth, run back
quickly to your spaceship
because you are nowhere
in the known universe!

TOP:
Nested Trapezoids.
R. Ausbourne, 2005.
Impossible squares do
not always have to have
four elements.

BOTTOM:
Square within a Square.
R. Ausbourne, 2005. An
impossible square within
a square. Can you find all
the twists?

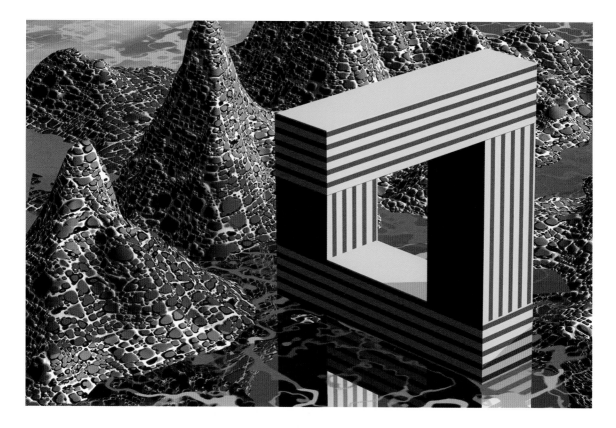

TOP:
Alien Trapezoid.
R. Ausbourne, 2005.
This 3-D figure could
never actually exist on
this planet.

BOTTOM:
Seaside Secret.
R. Ausbourne, 2007.

OPPOSITE:
Refreshments.
R. Ausbourne, 2005.
If you come upon this
concession stand in
the desert, just keep
crawling.

IMPOSSIBILITY IN ITS PUREST FORM: THE TRIANGLE

When British mathematician Roger Penrose called the impossible triangle design "impossibility in its purest form," he was referring to the simplicity of the design. So far, the impossible triangle is the simplest and most elegant impossible thing anyone has ever drawn.

The triangle is made up of only three bars. The design looks like a normal 3-D object at first, but if you examine the figure closely, you will notice that the bar that appears to extend toward you somehow joins with the bar extending away from you, even though they are both connected to the bar on the bottom.

The world's first impossible triangle design showed up on the sketchpad of Swedish artist Oscar Reutersvärd, who invented the design in 1934 during a train ride through the Swedish countryside. He started with a six-pointed star and placed solid 3-D cubes adjoining its inside crooks. The design became impossible when he placed cube number 6 behind cube number 1.

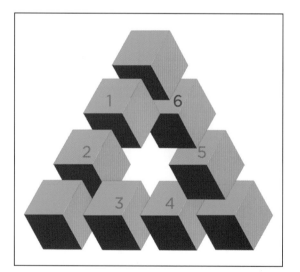

ABOVE LEFT:
Anatomy of the Tri-bar. R. Ausbourne, 2009. To make an impossible triangle, place solid cubes around a six-pointed star in the sequence shown. Place each cube so that it overlaps the last. Cube number 6 is the key to impossibility: Instead of overlapping cube number 1, it is tucked behind it. To complete a solid triangle, fill in all three corners with additional cubes, and then fill in the spaces between the cubes.

ABOVE RIGHT:
The Tri-bar As a 3-D Figure. R. Ausbourne, 2009. This is what the triangle would look like without the cube number 6 tuck trick. This triangle remains possible because cube number 6 now juts out in front of the structure, as it would in normal 3-D.

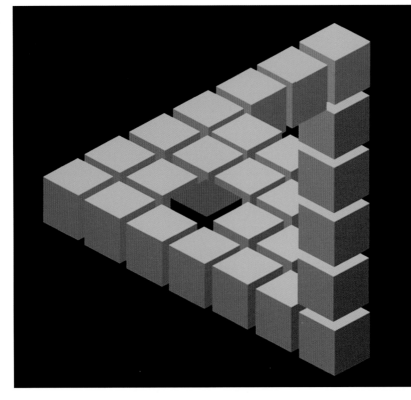

TOP:
Penrose. Josh
Sommers, 2008.
Artist's statement:
"Inspired by the classic
Penrose Triangle illusion,
recreated in 3-D."

BOTTOM:
*Design for Twenty-Six
Cubes.* R. Ausbourne,
2005. An impossible
triangle design made
from a matrix of cubes.

In a way, the triangle works just like a Möbius strip. The Möbius strip, named after nineteenth-century German mathematician August Ferdinand Möbius, has only one side and one edge, which you can create by adding a one-half twist to a strip of paper and joining the ends to form a loop. Many impossible objects have this same half-twist, yet the Möbius strip is not an impossible object. Make your own Möbius strip—it's easy!

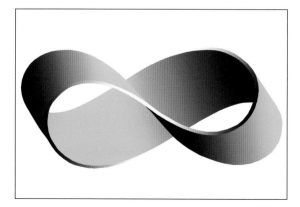

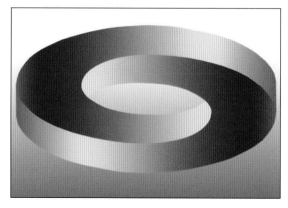

TWISTED FENCES

In the illustration *Offshore Habitat*, everything looks quite pleasant, but something is amiss. Two sets of horizontal poles punch through two vertical poles at two completely different angles. Because the sets of horizontal poles are oriented at a 90-degree angle with respect to each other, the ends of one set of horizontal poles can punch through one upright pole, but not both at the same time. The object lies frozen in the land of impossibility.

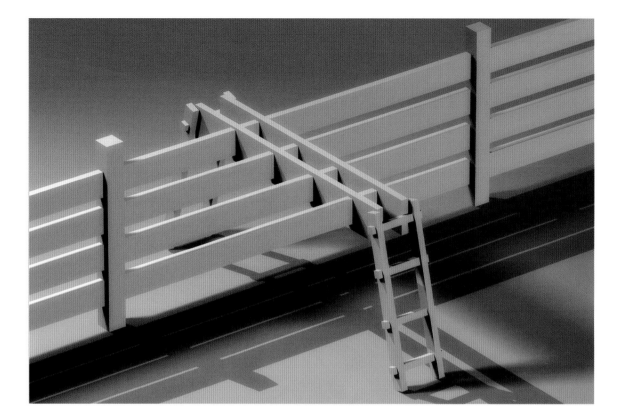

THE DEVIL'S FORK

TOP:

The Devil's Fork. Josh Sommers, 2008. Artist's statement: "The *Devil's Fork* illusion is one of the first illusions I remember seeing. I was fascinated by it as a child. Later, when I began to attempt to reproduce illusions and impossible objects in 3-D, it was one of the first I experimented with, and to this day it continues to be my favorite."

RIGHT:

A Tongue-in-Cheek Technical Diagram. R. Ausbourne, 1976. This plan contains a Devil's Fork, three impossible rings, and an impossible square. Can you find them all? Give this diagram to your tech department and watch the fun unfold!

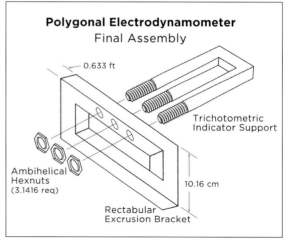

Polygonal Electrodynamometer
Final Assembly

0.633 ft

Trichotometric Indicator Support

Ambihelical Hexnuts (3.1416 req)

10.16 cm

Rectabular Excrusion Bracket

ABOVE:

Two Columns or Three? Josh Sommers, 2008. Artist's statement: "This illusion has always been one of my favorites. The particular rendition seen here was inspired by the work of American artist Walter Wick, who managed to build and photograph a 3-D model of this illusion using careful lighting and semi-reflective glass."

STAIRWAY TO NOWHERE

TOP:

Executive Ladder.
R. Ausbourne, 2005.
No matter how fast
or how far you climb,
you'll find you've been
there before.

OPPOSITE:

Tropical Improbable.
R. Ausbourne, 2005.
This diving platform is
giving tourists a lot of
trouble: The stairs lead
up to the same level!

BOTTOM:

Impossible Stairs.
R. Ausbourne, 2005.
Here is the impossible
staircase reduced to its
simplest form—three
steps in an endless
circle, going nowhere.
A subtle lie in the
geometry creates this
phenomenon. If you
were to view the model
straight on, you might
notice that the right-
hand sides slope down
ever so slightly in order
to meet steps on the
left—as is true for all
impossible stairways.

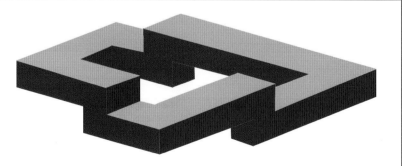

THE IMPOSSIBLE BOX

TOP:

Impossible Crate. Josh Sommers, 2008. Artist's statement: "This image was my first attempt at recreating a classic impossible object in three dimensions and helped me to establish the mind-set and technique that I used to create all of my other 3-D illusion experiments."

BOTTOM:

Inter-Cube.
R. Ausbourne, 2005. This cube design has a rather obvious impossibility. Note that many impossible objects are drawn using the angles of 90, 60, and 30 degrees, with a right-triangle tool. There is no horizon or vanishing point.

OPPOSITE:

Impossible Cube. Josh Sommers, 2008. Artist's statement: "Inspired by the classic impossible cube illustration, with this image I sought to recreate the illusion in a believable 3-D rendering, complete with reflection and shadow." *Note*: Inset shows a rare view of this unfinished box design.

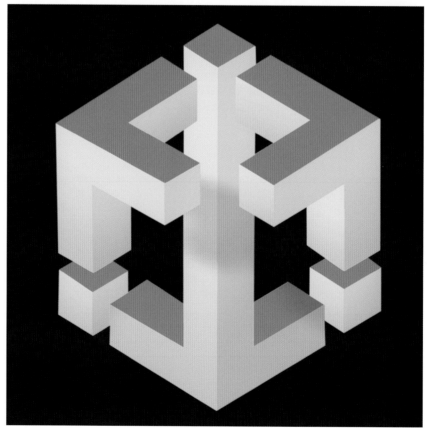

OTHER IMPOSSIBLE FIGURES

Impossible Structure.
Josh Sommers, 2008.
Artist's statement: "The impossible structure was an experiment to see how far I could push a perspective-based illusion in 3-D. My main intent was to discover how well others would recognize the impossibilities presented in a structure like this. I have found that many people do not immediately recognize the impossible aspects of this structure until they are asked to take a second look."

Impossible Pyramid.
Josh Sommers, 2008.

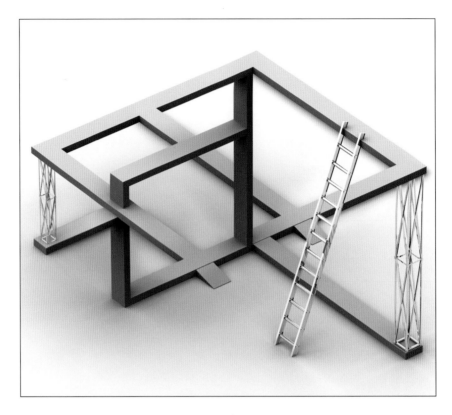

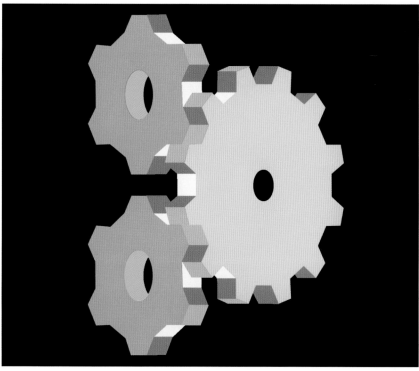

TOP:

Wheel Thing.
R. Ausbourne, 2009.
An homage to Swiss
artist Sandro Del-
Prete's classic drawing,
*Quadrature of the
Wheel.* You'll get no
work from this gizmo.

BOTTOM:

Gearosity. R. Ausbourne,
2005. Three interlocking
gears . . . not! The whole
thing is a watchmaker's
nightmare. The
three gears are not
interlocked; they are
embedded. Each gear
has cogs that share
contours with cogs on a
neighboring gear. None
of these gears can exist
without the others.

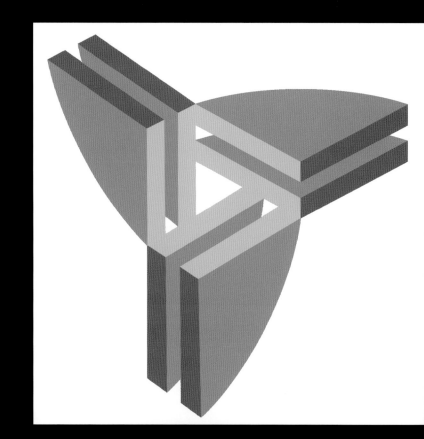

Design for Six Slices.
R. Ausbourne, 2005.
Don't try to build this
model in your shop:
The slices cannot be
grouped in this way.
At least one of the pairs
would have to overlap
with another pair.

Interlocking Batons.
R. Ausbourne, 2005.
Here we see a curious
design with six blue-
and-gold cylinders. Is
it impossible? If you
stare at the layout a bit,
it will begin to come
together. There are two
triangles composed
of three cylinders
woven together. These
identical triangles
appear completely
interlocked, with the
ends of each cylinder
touching another, but
this figure is impossible.
The ends only appear to
touch one another—in
actuality, they don't.

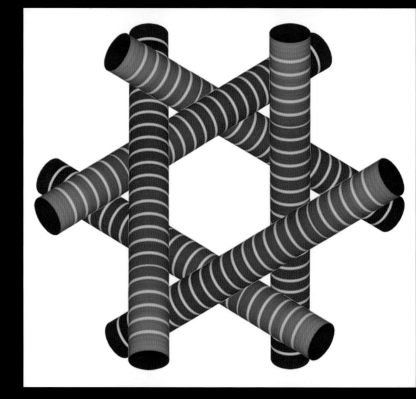

TOP:
Bent Straw.
R. Ausbourne, 2010. I once saw a trick pencil made out of rubber—this isn't one of those. I drew a straight straw, but it looks bent.

BOTTOM:
Four Sticks.
R. Ausbourne, 2005. This design hovers on the edge of impossibility. If the four sticks that pass through the central hub are continuous, then they must twist as they pass through it. If the sticks are not continuous, then an out-of-sight rotation and attachment can be suspected, making it possible to construct the model in 3-D.

ABOVE:

Satire on False Perspective. William Hogarth, 1753. The caption in this engraving reads, "Whoever makes a Design without the Knowledge of Perspective will be liable to such Absurdities as are shown in this Frontispiece." Hogarth is telling his students that mistakes in perspective may result in absurdities. How many impossible things can you spot?

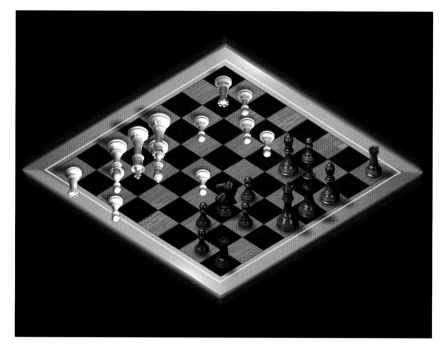

TOP:
Endless Chess.
R. Ausbourne, 2009.
This chessboard has trouble deciding whether it is right-side up or upside down, since both the top and bottom corners of the chessboard appear to be in the foreground. It is quite impossible.

BOTTOM:
Seaside and Easel.
R. Ausbourne, 2009.
Is the easel part of the scene, or is the scene part of the easel?

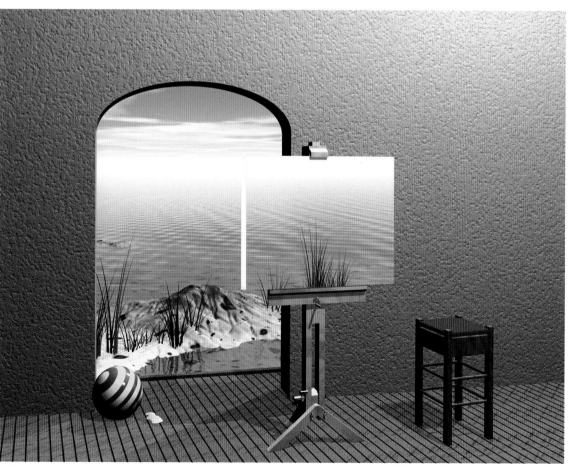

5

A DISTORTED WORLD

Five senses; an incurably abstract intellect; a haphazardly selective memory;
a set of preconceptions and assumptions so numerous that I can never examine
more than a minority of them—never become conscious of them all.
How much of total reality can such an apparatus let through?

—C. S. LEWIS (1898–1963)

have often compared human vision with a computerized imaging system because the similarities are useful in making the organic, flesh-and-blood vision process easier to grasp. However, it is important to keep in mind that there are insurmountable differences between an electronic replica and the miraculous network of human vision.

The processor in a top-of-the-line digital camera cannot hope to compete with that of a human being. In fact, the human brain uses almost half its total brainpower to accomplish the merest glance, which amounts to more processing power than all the supercomputers in the world put together. Our brains make independent, thoughtful assumptions about what we see; all we have to do is keep our eyes open. It is almost impossible to look at a tree and see it as something else. Our brains are hardwired to return a coherent, meaningful image; otherwise, we become delusional. Yet, in some cases, what our brain tells us about what we're seeing is different from what's in front of us. In other words, we see what our brains assume we should see, regardless of what is real.

Unless we are schizophrenic, lost in the desert, or under the influence of a hallucinogenic drug, it is not possible for us to see something that isn't there, but it is possible for the mind to make small, harmless assumptive errors. When induced, these are called *distortion illusions*. What I find

OPPOSITE:
Gonzo Ponzo.
R. Ausbourne, 2008.
The white parallel lines that extend above and below horizon lines appear to be of a consistent length. However, those white lines intersecting the horizon lines appear longer because they are influenced by an erroneous internal assumption. All the horizontal lines that are in the central column are the same length.

interesting about distortion illusions is that once you reach closure with a distortion illusion and realize that a line really isn't bent, it still looks bent! To an artist, this is staggering. I drew that line straight—I know I did! But the line looked bent as soon as I drew it and will remain so for all viewers until the end of time.

The Bent Square illusion is a good example of an assumptive visual error. The square looks bent, even though it isn't. The mind is greatly influenced by the circles under the square and cannot help but assume that the square is bent in comparison. As innocent bystanders, we are forced to see what the mind has assumed. If we were to remove the circles, the square would "unbend itself."

A ruler or straightedge will be useful throughout this section. You may be told often that this or that element is not bent, or that a certain line or space is shorter or longer. Just take my word for it, or find out for yourself using a straightedge. A good rule to follow: Question everything.

RIGHT:
Bent Square.
R. Ausbourne, 2008.

OPPOSITE, BOTTOM LEFT:
Chevron Distortion.
R. Ausbourne, 2008.
A battle of shapes, and this time the chevron's stripes appear to pull the circle out of shape. The circle is perfectly round—really!

OPPOSITE, BOTTOM RIGHT:
Bowed Distortion.
R. Ausbourne, 2011.
The red horizontal lines are straight, but the background figure is distorting them. The radiating lines are making them appear to bend.

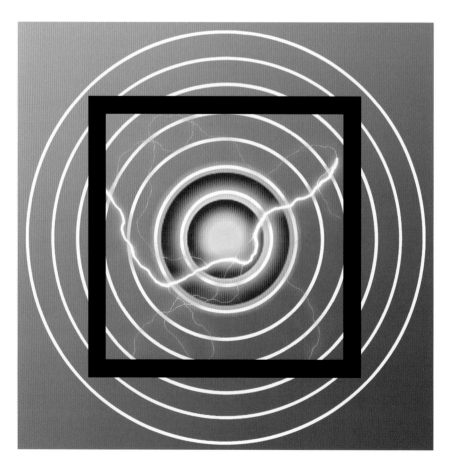

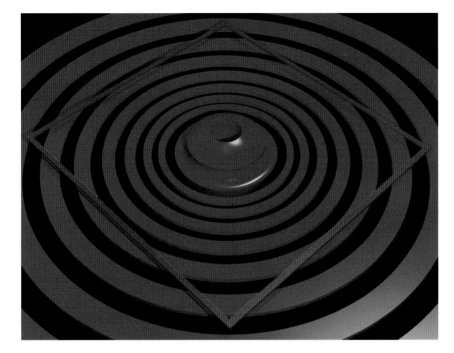

LEFT:
3-D Circles and Square.
R. Ausbourne, 2008.
This figure is the *Bent Square* illusion in 3-D. The sides of the square are not curved, yet the circle shapes behind appear to pull the square's sides inward.

CENTER LEFT:
Subjective Bent Square.
R. Ausbourne, 2007.

CENTER RIGHT:
Power Bars.
R. Ausbourne, 2007.
The diagonal bars that appear slightly bowed are actually straight.

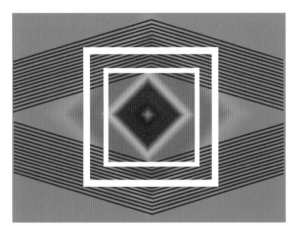

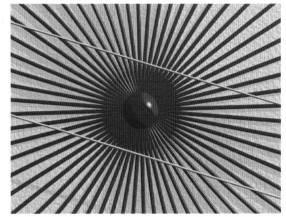

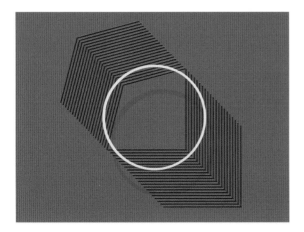

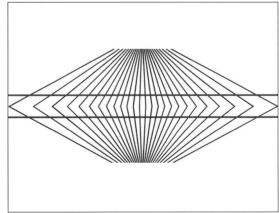

THE ILLUSION OF PERSPECTIVE

In the *Ponzo* illusion, the horizon lines look like railroad tracks extending into the distance. The mind readily places the parallel horizontal lines into the scene, comparing them to railroad ties. Yet if these lines were railroad ties, they would appear smaller in the distance. In other words, we interpret the top horizontal line as being farther away from us, so we expect it to be shorter in length than the line near the bottom of the image. Because the top line defies our expectations and is clearly *not* shorter than the bottom line, we actually perceive it as being *longer*. In fact, the two "railroad ties" are exactly the same length. Scientists call this illusion *inappropriate constancy scaling*.

RIGHT:
Ponzo.
R. Ausbourne, 2011.

OPPOSITE, BOTTOM:
An Illusion of Perspective.
R. Ausbourne, 2008.
The two images are identical. What is making them appear so different? Our sense of perspective struggles to incorporate the images into a single scene, even though there are two suns in the sky. Our brains naturally assume that everything must recede toward a single point on the horizon, and, thus, the angle of the horizon lines in one image appear to differ from that of the adjoining, identical image.

LEFT:

Metropolis.
R. Ausbourne, 2008.
It may be easier for us
to see the perspective
distortion illusion in
these two identical
skyscrapers. The
building on the right
seems to lean more than
its double on the left.
However, the buildings
rise before us at an
identical angle.

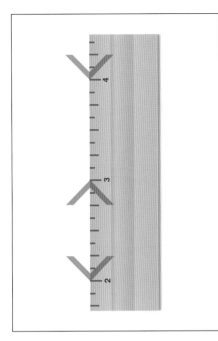

A similar trick is found in the *Müller-Lyer* illusion, first introduced by Franz Müller-Lyer in 1889. In this illusion we see an outside corner of a building and an inside corner scene placed side by side for comparison. Which of the two vertical red lines is longer? They are, in fact, the same length.

LEFT:
Pinched Inch.
R. Ausbourne, 2007.
In this variation of the *Müller-Lyer* illusion, reversed arrowheads are used, but they are shown along a portion of a ruler. Here, we cannot help but perceive that one inch is shorter than the other.

OPPOSITE:
Proboscidean Distortion.
R. Ausbourne, 2008.
The two elephants in this scene are the same size. The sloping walls and path cause a size consistency error similar to that in the Ponzo Illusion.

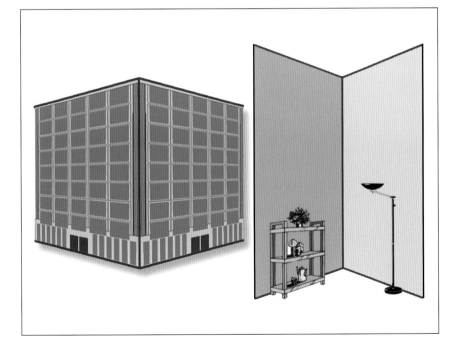

ABOVE:
Müller-Lyer. R. Ausbourne, 2005.
The elements in this illusion are very similar to familiar building structures, such as an exterior corner of a building and an interior corner of a room. The mind assumes that we must be closer to the walls in the interior view, which opens toward us, than we are to the building, so we assume that the red vertical line on the image at right must be longer than the red vertical line on the image at left.

WHERE'S THE CENTER?

Every shape we see or visualize has two centers: an *actual* center and a *visual* center. The first is an object's true geometric center, and the second merely appears to be its center. Using a simple equilateral triangle, we can illuminate the difference between the two centers, which is the result of a distortion illusion.

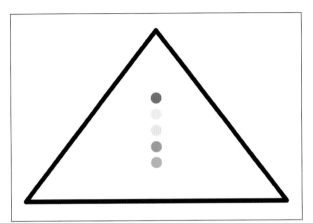

The yellow dot is not in the center of the triangle, although it appears to be. The actual center—the point that is equidistant between the top and bottom of the triangle—is represented by the light blue dot. Use a ruler to prove it! If the shape were a square, the actual and visual centers would overlap. This distortion will not work on shapes that are symmetrical across both a horizontal and a vertical axis.

TOP LEFT:
Equilateral Triangle. R. Ausbourne, 2008. Which dot is closest to the center of the triangle? If you chose the light blue dot, you are correct.

BOTTOM LEFT:
Lincoln's Hat. R. Ausbourne, 2011. The rule of intersecting lines is shown in an illusion called the *Lincoln's Hat* illusion, sometimes called the *Stove Pipe* illusion. The hat is as tall as it is wide at the brim. You can use your ruler to prove it.

ABOVE:
Rule of Intersecting Lines. R. Ausbourne, 2007. There is a rule of drawing that says a line segment that intersects another line segment of equal length will appear longer in comparison. This image illustrates the rule and the illusion. Line (a) is the same length as line (b).

OPPOSITE:
Pyramid of Deception. R. Ausbourne, 2005. The eyeball is exactly halfway up the pyramid.

A PROBLEM OF COMPARISON

Many optical illusions are caused by the way we compare objects to other objects in their immediate surroundings. The *Titchener Illusion*, introduced by nineteenth-century British psychologist Edward Bradford Titchener, is a comparison illusion.

We are very good at comparing sizes of objects in local groups, but not so good when it comes to comparing sizes of similar objects in separate groups, even when they are near each other. We judge the size of each red ball in comparison to its immediate neighbors, and this judgment of "large" or "small" easily supersedes our judgment of the size of one red ball as compared to the other.

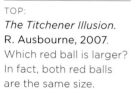

TOP:
The Titchener Illusion.
R. Ausbourne, 2007.
Which red ball is larger?
In fact, both red balls
are the same size.

BOTTOM:
Titchener in Crystal.
R. Ausbourne, 2009.
Another version of the
Titchener Illusion. The
two rose crystal balls
may look different,
due to the shadows
reflected from their
surfaces and the sizes
of the surrounding
cannonballs, but they
are the same size.

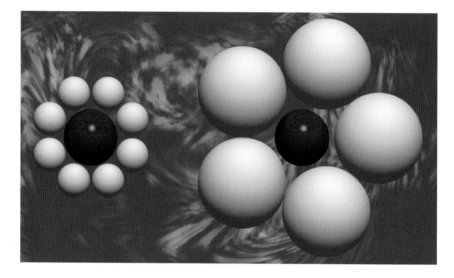

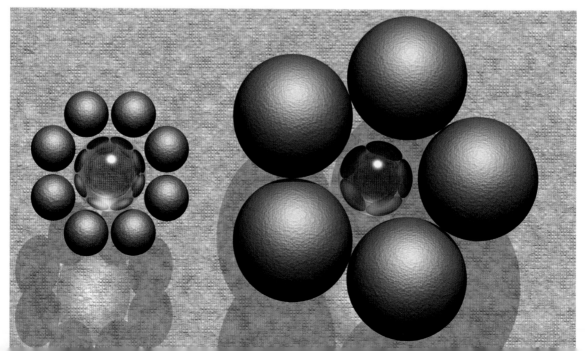

The *Banana Card* illusion illustrates how we sometimes compare and confuse the size of things. The two slanting cards are identical, but they are placed side by side in such a way as to force an assumptive error. If you place the shapes so that matching long or short curves are next to each other, the illusion of contrasting size does not occur.

TOP RIGHT:
Banana Card.
R. Ausbourne, 2011. The long curve of one shape is purposely placed next to the short curve of the opposite shape. We can't help but compare these curves, and the result is a generalization that one banana card must be slightly larger.

CENTER:
Sine Wave Effect. R. Ausbourne, 2008. The tiny vertical lines are all the same length, yet they give the impression that they vary in length throughout.

LEFT:
Wild Waveforms.
R. Ausbourne, 2008.

THE TROUBLE WITH DIAGONALS

The *Poggendorff Illusion* is named after German physicist Johann Christian Poggendorff, who introduced the illusion in 1860. Poggendorff was studying how we perceive diagonal lines in relation to intersecting horizontal and vertical lines. He showed that we are pretty good at tracking the path of a line across a gap, but not so good if the lines are diagonal. The following figure shows the classic Poggendorff illusion. When the colored lines are horizontal, we have very little trouble identifying which line is continuous beyond the gray gap. The trouble begins when the lines run at a diagonal.

OPPOSITE:

Ode to Poggendorff.
R. Ausbourne, 2008.
(Background painting by C. H. Brittenham.)
The red line appears as though it is continuous. It is not. The green segment actually lines up with the red segment on the left.

RIGHT:

Classic Poggendorff.
R. Ausbourne, 2008.
Which color line segment most closely lines up with the white segment on the left? If you chose the blue segment, look again! Yellow is the correct answer. A ruler will prove it.

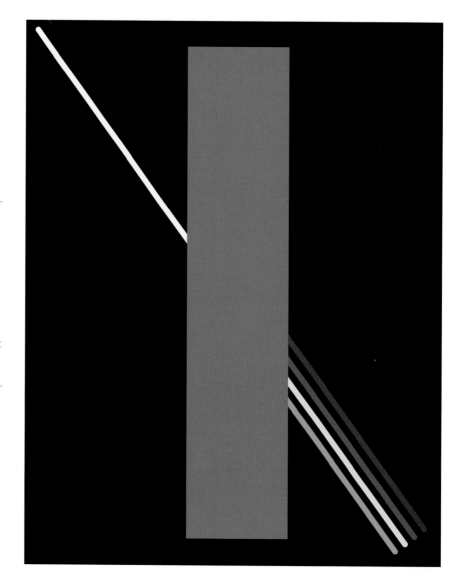

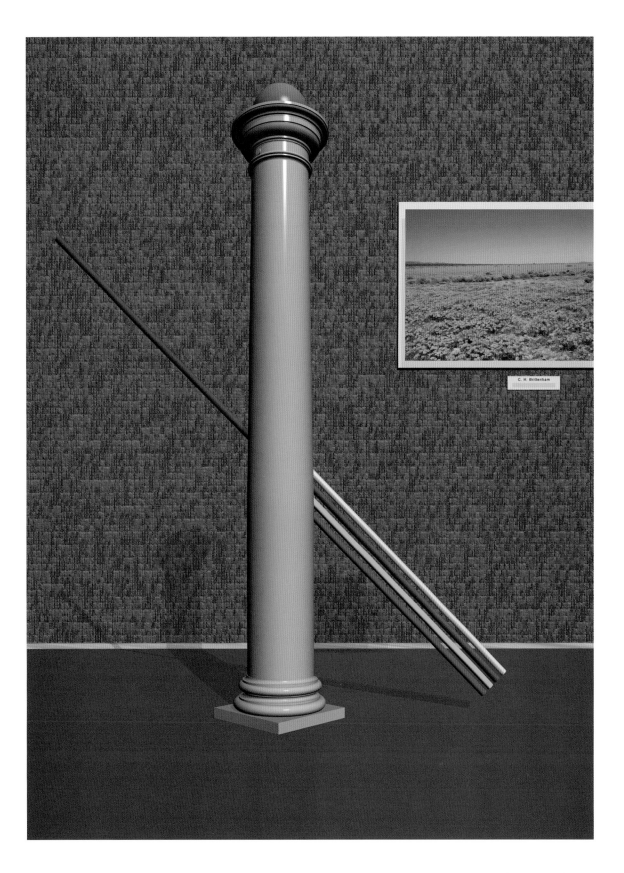

C. H. Brittenham

The *Chains and Board* illusion is a variation of the *Poggendorff Illusion*. Here, the gap is slightly wider and a continuous chain spans the gap. Do the chain lengths on each side of the board appear to meet each other behind it, proving the chain's continuity?

TOP:
Chains and Board.
R. Ausbourne, 2007.
The length of chain is continuous and meets the other half behind the board.

BOTTOM:
Distorted Step Plate.
R. Ausbourne, 2011.
This treaded step plate is being distorted by a few distracting triangle shapes placed at the corners. For some reason, we cannot quite grasp the plate as a uniform hexagon shape behind the triangles.

The *Zöllner Illusion* was originated by nineteenth-century German astrophysicist Johann Karl Freidrich Zöllner. The figure on the top left of the next page shows a series of diagonal lines placed in a simple herringbone pattern. If the intersecting lines run only vertically or only horizontally, there is no effect. However, when you reverse the direction of intersecting lines in alternate rows, a distortion occurs between the lines of the pattern. Another example shows this distortion using alternating patterns and text.

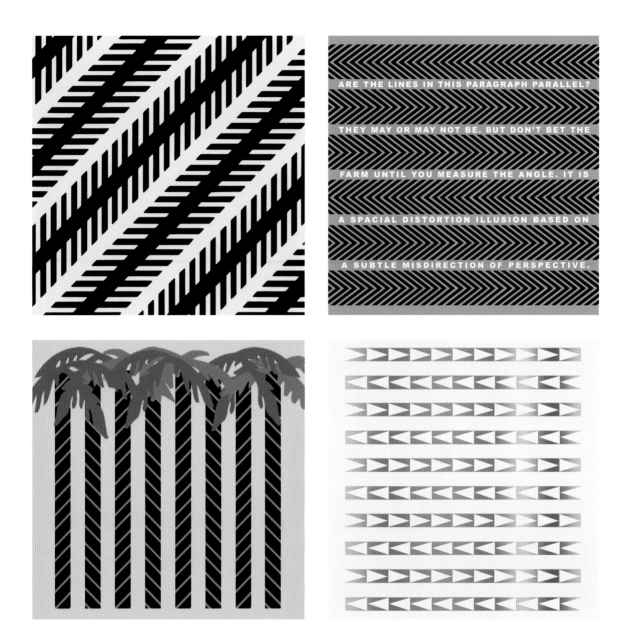

The image contains the text: ARE THE LINES IN THIS PARAGRAPH PARALLEL? THEY MAY OR MAY NOT BE. BUT DON'T BET THE FARM UNTIL YOU MEASURE THE ANGLE. IT IS A SPACIAL DISTORTION ILLUSION BASED ON A SUBTLE MISDIRECTION OF PERSPECTIVE.

TOP LEFT:
Zöllner Illusion.
R. Ausbourne, 2007.

TOP RIGHT:
Zöllner Distortion.
R. Ausbourne, 2007. In this horizontal pattern of Zöllner stripes, are the lines of text parallel? Use your ruler.

BOTTOM LEFT:
Zöllner Palm Grove.
R. Ausbourne, 2008. These palms are perfectly straight up and down. Alternating diagonal patterns have been added between their trunks, causing each tree to take an illusory lean to the right or left.

BOTTOM RIGHT:
Indian Blanket Distortion.
R. Ausbourne, 2008. The motif in this distortion effect appears to narrow slightly in the opposite direction of the arrowhead symbols. Notice that the design is full of alternating herringbone patterns. Zöllner has struck again!

Fraser's Spiral illusion is a cousin of the *Zöllner Illusion*. It is often called the *Twisted Cord* illusion because of a braided effect within the "spirals." However, this image is not a spiral at all. In truth, it is made up of concentric circles radiating outward from the center. The illusion is caused by the ropy design inside the circles.

RIGHT:
Fraser's Spiral. James Fraser, 1908. This amazing distortion was first published in the 1908 edition of the *British Journal of Psychology*, along with a description by James Fraser.

ABOVE LEFT:
Braided Text.
R. Ausbourne, 2008. Here is a twist on *Fraser's Spiral.* The individual letters for the word *LIFE* in this design are actually straight. The braided effect makes them look crooked. Only a ruler will prove otherwise.

ABOVE RIGHT:
Simple Twist.
R. Ausbourne, 2008. Here is a simplified version of *Fraser's Spiral.* The first row has red guidelines added to demonstrate that the patterns are actually parallel. Each pattern is alternately reversed so that they appear to zigzag from top to bottom.

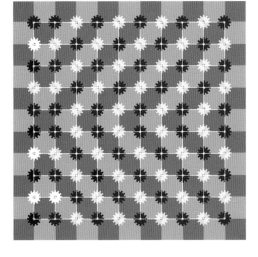

Café Wall.
R. Ausbourne, 2008.
This tilting pattern of tiles is not tilting at all. The illusion was first noticed on a tiled café wall in England, in the 1970s, and first described by Richard L. Gregory and Priscilla Heard at the University of Bristol. Ordinary tile work does not cause such an illusion. This illusion is caused by the thickness and shade of the grout, plus the amount of offset given to the tiled layers.

ILLUSORY CONTOURS

LEFT:

Optical Aberration.
R. Ausbourne, 2009.
One gear placed on the board would make little difference, but an aggregate of gears in contrasting colors distorts the symmetry of the checkerboard pattern.

BOTTOM:

Where Is the Light Coming From? R. Ausbourne, 2007. We are used to seeing the reflection of light emanating from above us. This notion is so strong that it is almost impossible to overcome. The three sections in this illustration with light tops look like humps, while the three with dark tops look like hollows. Try to imagine that the reverse is true—that light comes from the bottom and that the humps and hollows are reversed.

TOP:

Distorted Checkerboard. R. Ausbourne, 2011.
This checkerboard appears at first to be distorted, but it's not. Each of the overlaid elements has very little effect individually, but together they produce a considerable effect. Grab a ruler and see for yourself.

BOTTOM:

Stars and Squares. R. Ausbourne, 2009.
This is a normal checkerboard that is being visually distorted by stars placed strategically among the rows.

OPPOSITE:

Mystic Wheel. R. Ausbourne, 2008.
Everything in this design is 2-D: The wavy spokes are identical and flat, the background is uniformly black, and the marble in the center has no effect on the illusion. Nevertheless, the wheel appears to have 3-D ripples radiating out from its center. No matter how you rotate the design, the humps and hollows of the ripples remain. Perhaps this happens because we tend to think of light as coming from above.

THE PERSISTENCE
OF VISION

I stop looking, but my eyes keep going!

—ROBERT AUSBOURNE

Afterimages are working residue left on the retina from the act of seeing. Images do not wash off the retina right away; they tend to hang around a bit. We are normally unaware of afterimages, however, because our eyes are continuously moving, replacing images with other images. Afterimages can be a fun and often enlightening phenomenon of the visual system to explore. It's easy to visualize them: You simply look at something and then stop and let your eyes and mind do the rest.

The lore of afterimages begins in the sixteenth century, when a French scientist by the name of Chevalier Patrice d'Arcy decided to tie a glowing lump of coal to the end of a wire and swing it around in the dark. He noticed that the movement of the lump of coal produced a trail of light, just as modern sparklers do today when we wave them around in the dark. D'Arcy reasoned that the eye must retain an image for a short length of time, and that if the *next* image is similar and arrives quickly enough, the result is a continuous string of images that smear together in a kind of mini–light show. He called this phenomenon the *persistence of vision*. In modern times experiments with persistence of vision have enabled us to watch TV, digital movies, and IMAX films.

Anyone who has ever been in front of a camera when a camera flash goes off has seen an example of the persistence of vision. That brief moment just after the flash, when you blink your eyes and it takes a few seconds to

OPPOSITE:
Persistence of Vision.
R. Ausbourne, 2009.
Glowing sparklers create incandescent trails in the darkness as long chains of movielike images persist in the mind's eye.

recover, is an extreme example of an afterimage. The afterimage illusions you will see here are kinder and much gentler.

In order to visualize an afterimage illusion, you first have to charge up your photoreceptors. In other words, you need to collect enough visual imagery to give a specific set of photoreceptors a really good look at the scene. Try not to move your eyes while you are charging up. Each time you move your eyes, even a little, a new set of receptors gets involved and you will need to start all over again. The technique I use for charging is something I call the *million-mile stare*.

I invoke the million-mile stare by imagining myself as a child in summer school listening to a teacher drone on endlessly about intransitive verbs or some other virtually useless subject. I imagine myself staring lazily out a window at nothing at all—and everything, at once. My eyes are motionless—focused—but not seeing anything specific. I am taking in the whole scene and my mind is a million miles away. Some people might call this an *expansive stare*, or just plain spacey. Whatever you call it, the technique works great for afterimages. You can use your own method— perhaps the *zombie stare* or the *robot face*. Use whatever technique works best for you.

The length of time required to charge up photoreceptors varies with the scene you are taking in. The afterimages in this chapter will not require charge times of over thirty seconds—any longer, and the results aren't worth the trouble. A good afterimage will have a minimum charge time and maximum effect. Once you have completed the charging process, direct your attention to any nearby neutral surface, such as a blank sheet of paper, a light desk surface, or a wall. Try closing your eyes. The backs of your eyelids are dark, so if the object or scene is white, you will lose

A WORD OF CAUTION

Your eyes will eagerly accept light energy from whatever source you are looking at without warning bells. If you stare at the sun, your retinas will happily accept a torrent of input and allow a few billion electromagnetic photons to *cook your eyeballs like a TV dinner!* (Don't do it.) If you cannot see afterimages, don't worry about it. Individual differences, such as color blindness and light sensitivity, may be limiting factors. Working in dim light may produce weak effects and may cause eyestrain. Be sure to try these experiments using adequate lighting.

it when your eyes are shut. Afterimages usually occur in the opposite or complementary colors of the original scene. A black scene will produce a white afterimage. A handy color wheel showing twelve common colors and their complementary afterimage colors is provided below.

The fact that afterimages usually occur in a complementary color is not fully understood. A common belief is that photoreceptors for a particular color become fatigued and emit weak signals, while surrounding photo-receptors emit stronger signals, generating the complementary color when our eyes move away from the stimulus and onto a neutral, light surface.

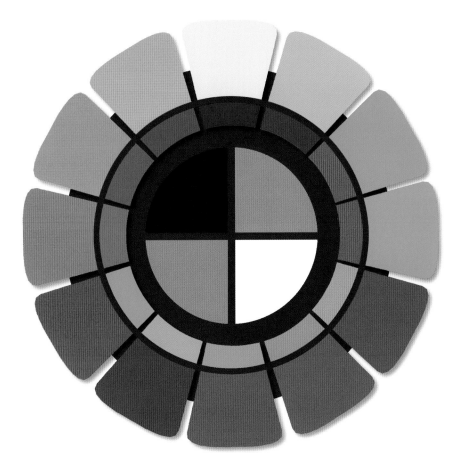

LEFT:

Afterimage Color Wheel. R. Ausbourne, 2009. This color wheel can be used to identify twelve major complementary color pairs. The inner wheel shows colors that are produced in afterimages by objects in colors on the outer wheel. Colors are approximate, as afterimages are wispy and usually light in hue. Notice that the afterimage of 50 percent black is 50 percent white and that these colors are identical. For this reason, gray is often used as a background color for afterimage illusions.

Now that we know what they are and how to see them, let's test our million-mile stare on a simple black-and-white afterimage illusion. To see this afterimage, you should stare at the black dot on the left for about fifteen seconds. However, you can develop a dim effect in as little as five seconds. Once you are charged up, shift your gaze to the black square on the right. What do you see?

You should see a wispy gray dot floating in the black square. The dot will be brighter depending on how long you stared at the black dot and how adequate the lighting is where you performed the experiment.

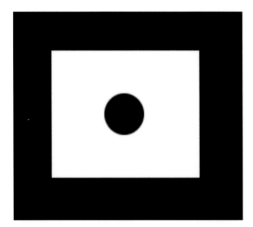

COLOR COMPLEMENTS

Now we are ready to try our technique with color. The next afterimage illusion shows a traffic light with the wrong colors. To see the correct

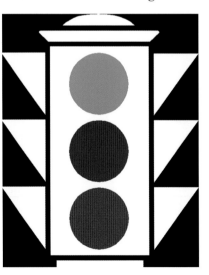

colors, stare at the center (blue) light for about fifteen seconds, or a bit longer if needed. Look at a neutral surface, and an afterimage of the standard traffic light colors should appear.

The figure on the opposite page is a full-page rendering of the same illusion for those who wish to practice their million-mile stare from across the room.

A DISAPPEARING ACT

The afterimage effect of the *Disappearing Clouds* illusion will happen while you are charging. To make the clouds disappear, stare at the black dot and watch out of the corner of your eyes (peripheral vision) as the clouds disappear little by little until they are all gone. The colors will usually fade within about ten seconds. If you move your eyes, the clouds will reappear. What is happening here?

Photoreceptors require charged particles to do their jobs. As you look at the illusion, working photoreceptors run low on photosensitive calcium ions and cyclic nucleotides through the process of neural adaptation, so the colors start to fade. If you move your eyes, the colors reappear as sensitive, "fresh" photoreceptors go to work. Photoreceptors can instantly regain sensitivity and go back to work, but not while you are using them. Note that the background color, 50 percent gray, does not appear to fade or change color. It does fade, but the afterimage of 50 percent gray is 50 percent gray.

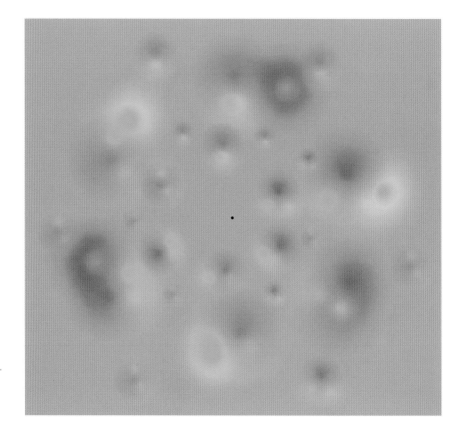

RIGHT:
Disappearing Clouds.
A. Azevedo, 2009.

PERIPHERAL GHOSTS

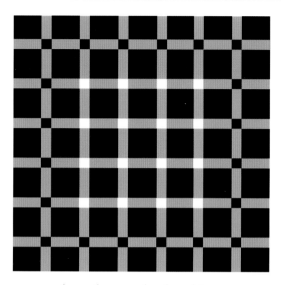

The *Foggy Blue Bottom Fuzz* illusion works as soon as you look at it. No charging necessary. The illusion occurs in your peripheral vision rather than your direct line of sight.

The blue tint is an afterimage illusion of the adjoining yellow rectangles. The black squares throughout make the white squares appear brighter. The blue tint doesn't appear in a square you are looking at because, in your direct line of sight, working photoreceptors identify the correct color. Nearby white squares in your peripheral vision are where afterimages may occur.

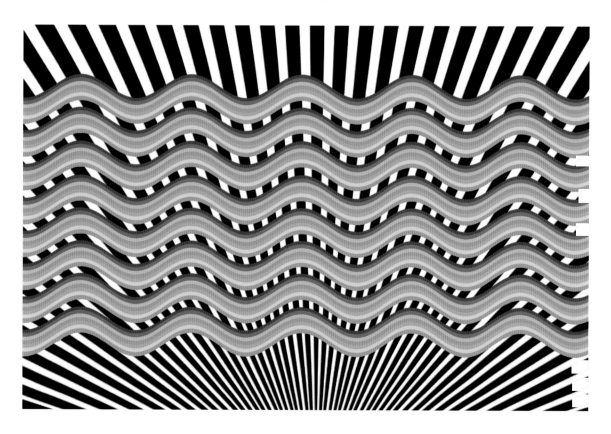

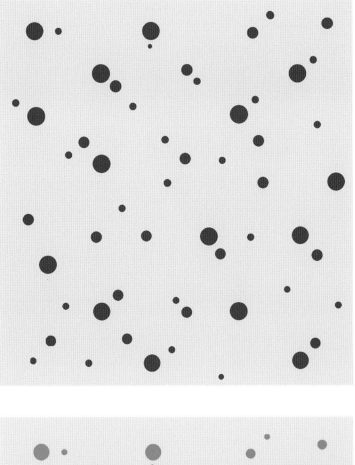

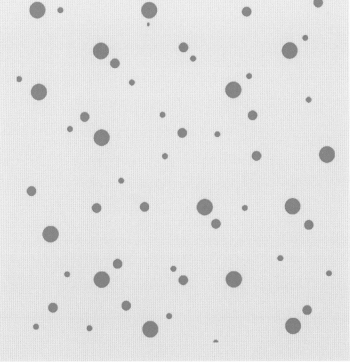

TOP LEFT:

Blue Dots. R. Ausbourne, 2007. Look at any blue dot for about three seconds, and then move your eyes very slightly in any direction. A matching pattern of yellow afterimages floats nearby. As it fades, pause and look at another blue dot. Yellow and blue are complements. Again, neutral gray has been used for the background color.

BOTTOM LEFT:

Mystery Dot Quiz. R. Ausbourne, 2007. This afterimage illusion is similar to the previous example, but, in this example, the afterimage color is a complete mystery until you try it. Do you know what the afterimage color will be? Consulting the *Afterimage Color Wheel* is perfectly okay. The answer can be found on page 150.

OPPOSITE:

Particle Accelerator. R. Ausbourne, 2008. Bright colors and high-contrast patterns cause this design to come alive with flashing afterimage illusions. Keep your eyes moving across the image, and you will see shadows race around the circular forms. These afterimages move at the speed of thought.

FUN WITH AFTERIMAGES

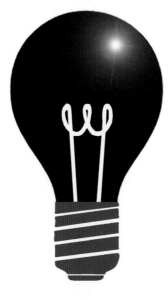

TOP RIGHT:

Lightbulb Afterimage.
R. Ausbourne, 2008.
This incandescent
lightbulb can be
illuminated with the
power of an afterimage.
Stare at the filament for
about fifteen to twenty-
five seconds, and then
stare at a blank sheet of
paper or any convenient
neutral light-colored
surface. You should see
a white bulb and black
filament with a brassy/
orange-colored base.
The reflective glow on
the bulb will turn black.

CENTER RIGHT:

Old Glory. R. Ausbourne,
2007. This illusion is
an image of Old Glory.
All hail the Green,
Black, and Orange!
Hey—that's not right.
This afterimage show
requires about a
twenty-second charge.

BOTTOM RIGHT:

Green Imp. Anonymous.
The *Green Imp* is an
afterimage from a time
when imps were part of
popular culture. Imps
were not considered
evil—merely obnoxious
. . . and green. How can
we make this red imp
turn green?

BOTTOM LEFT:
Alien Pumpkin.
R. Ausbourne, 2003.
I don't know about you, but I've never seen a pumpkin like this on planet Earth. Stare into its menacing eyes for about fifteen seconds to see its true colors.

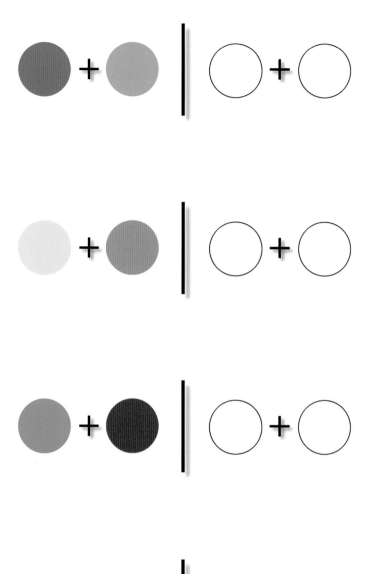

RIGHT:

Afterimage Field Test.
R. Ausbourne, 2009.
Try to guess what the
afterimage color pairs
will be for each of these
examples. Charge up
your photoreceptors
by staring at the cross
symbol between the
two test colors on
the left for about
ten seconds. Then
shift your gaze to the
opposite cross to see
an afterimage.
See page 150 for the
answers.

NAME THAT LUMINARY

TOP LEFT:
I Have a Dream.
R. Ausbourne, 2009.
This is a drawing of a
famous American. Can
you tell who it is? Give
it about a fifteen-
second charge.
See page 150 for
the answer.

CENTER LEFT:
Italian Navigator.
R. Ausbourne, 2007. In
1492, this person sailed
the ocean blue. Can you
name him? Give it about
a fifteen-second charge.
See page 150 for
the answer.

BOTTOM LEFT:
*Good-bye Norma
Jean.* R. Ausbourne,
2010. This Illusion is
an homage to a movie
star whose "candle
burned out long before
[her] legend ever did,"
according to rock
singer Elton John.
Can you identify the
popular star?
See page 150 for
the answer.

RIGHT, TOP TO BOTTOM:
Historical Figures 1. How
many of these historical
figures can you identify
by visualizing the
afterimages? Give
each about a fifteen-
second charge.
See page 150 for the
answers.

LEFT, TOP TO BOTTOM:
Historical Figures 2.
How many of these
historical figures
can you identify
by examining their
afterimages? Give each
about a fifteen-second
charge. See page 150
for the answers.

RIGHT, TOP TO BOTTOM:
Historical Figures 3.
How many of these
historical figures can you
identify by visualizing
these afterimages? Give
each about a fifteen-
second charge.
See page 150 for the
answers.

LEFT, TOP TO BOTTOM:
Historical Figures 4.
How many of these
historical figures can you
identify by visualizing
the afterimages? Give
each about a fifteen-
second charge.
See page 150 for the
answers.

NATURE'S ILLUSIONS

Camouflage: k m' fläzh
From Parisian street slang, camoufler: "to disguise,"
naturalized during World War I to camouflage: to disguise
by artificial means or to blend into one's surroundings.

The term *camouflage* was introduced by the French during World War I, when they were developing schemes to conceal military assets. Modern military camouflage uniforms employ colorful camouflage patterns that enable soldiers to blend into the colors and textures of almost any environment. Camouflage color schemes use the three or four most common colors in a local environment, so the odds are pretty good that the uniform will match at least one or two of them. Camouflaged uniforms give an enemy very little to focus on. Expected contours, borders, colors, textures, and even mass are broken and confused.

OPPOSITE:
Zebra Code.
Anonymous. This whimsical design of a zebra against a barcode shows how vertical lines break up the contours of the zebra.

LEFT:
Artificial Camouflage Patterns. R. Ausbourne, 2008. Modern combat units can be camouflaged to match a variety of terrains.

THE OLD RAZZLE DAZZLE

Razzle dazzle or *dazzle paint* are naval terms applied to a camouflage scheme used not for concealment, but rather as a way to confuse

enemy spotters. Paint jobs on navy ships during World War I consisted of random patterns of bold stripes and shapes in contrasting colors. From a distance, it was difficult to judge the course and speed of a dazzle-painted ship and even harder to tell whether a ship was moving toward or away from the observer. In the time it took to identify the course of the target, a razzle-dazzle ship could slip out of range. Dazzle-painting was abandoned during World War II when radar was developed, which greatly reduced the effectiveness of such elaborate paint schemes.

OPPOSITE:
U.S. Marine in Afghanistan.
A U.S. Marine stands guard in Afghanistan, wearing standard-issue military combat fatigues.

TOP:
USS *Orizaba in 1918, Shown with Razzle Dazzle Camouflage.*

BOTTOM:
USS *Charles S. Sperry.* This American warship is seen displaying a coat of 3-D razzle-dazzle designs near the Statue of Liberty in 1944.

ADAPTIVE COLORATION

In the animal kingdom, many species have evolved adaptive coloration for the purpose of warning, visual deception, camouflage, mimicry, or just plain bravado. For example, the Tawny Frogmouth bird shown below sits absolutely still on her nest in the Australian rain forest—even her eyes are closed to complete her camouflage scheme. It is difficult for predators to decide where the bird ends and the branch begins.

Camouflage evolves in nature to help species blend into the natural environment. Individual species themselves have no real choice in the matter; the evolutionary process is long and gradual, as the members with the most advantageous physical markings simply survive long enough to produce offspring that exhibit similar camouflage patterns. Take a look at the leaf frog on the opposite page—if you can find the little well-camouflaged amphibian. Give up? Follow the thick branch to its broken end. The frog is a khaki-colored blob sitting upright, facing the branch from below. This little frog lives in a place where, if you don't blend into the background, you get eaten.

Genetic mutations occur from time to time in the natural world. Some mutations are good and some are bad. At some point, a frog will be born that happens to look a little more like a leaf than other frogs—a *good* genetic mutation. The mutant leafy-looking frog blends into the background better than the other frogs and is more likely to live long enough to mate. Leafy-looking frogs produce even leafier frogs, and, eventually, the leafiest frogs will replace all frogs of this species. This process—as old as life itself—is

OPPOSITE:
Leaf Frog. A frog is camouflaged in the leafy forest litter of its environment. Can you find this little critter?

ABOVE:
Tawny Frogmouth. This bird (*Podargus strigoides*) from the Australian rain forest holds perfectly still and blends into its indigenous environment.

called *natural selection*. It favors many tiny, successful mutations over a huge span of time. Mother Nature selects those mutations that help a species survive. Because leafy-looking frogs are less likely to be consumed by predators, she favors them over other frog species.

How the Zebra Got Its Stripes. R. Ausbourne, 2007. Imagine yourself as a hungry lion. You are naturally color-blind and see mostly in black and white. You are stalking zebra, but their stripes break up their outlines in the tall grass—it is hard to tell what is zebra and what is not. Be patient and watch the herd closely. Careful, the one you are after may escape notice!

PREDATORS, PREY, AND THE VISION GAP

Predatory animals often have better vision than prey because they have been selected for enhanced visual acuity in order to overcome effective camouflage on their hunting grounds. We humans are at the top of the food chain, which easily explains why we devote almost half our brainpower to vision. However, our sight is no match for the eyes of an eagle, which relies exclusively on its ability to discern small creatures from a high altitude in order to grab a meal. For every improvement in effective camouflage, there has also been a step forward in visual acuity, resulting in a billion-year biological race between predator and prey.

TOP:
Giant Treefrog (Hypsiboas boans). This camouflaged frog is almost indistinguishable from its environment. If the environment changes too fast, this frog may not have time to adapt and runs the risk of extinction.

CENTER:
Dead Leaf Mantis (Deroplatys desiccata). This mantis from Madagascar is not dead, but it plays the part of a dead leaf in life.

BOTTOM:
Red Milk and Coral Snakes. One of these snakes is highly venomous, and the other is harmless. Which one is which? It is best to avoid both. That is exactly what the harmless red milk snake on the right is counting on by being a clever mimic.

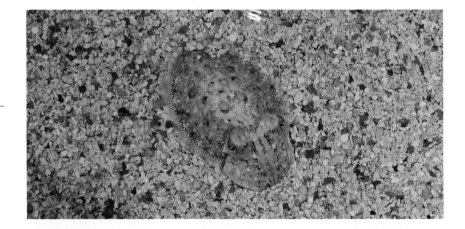

Mimicry is not limited to the animal kingdom. Some plants mimic other species to intimidate predators or increase cultivation. One example of plant mimicry is the common rye plant.

THE SAMURAI CRAB

Every species can recognize its fellow members, and we are no exception. We begin to recognize facial features as soon as we enter the world. Facial *expressions* are a whole other matter; we wrestle with them all our lives.

There is an interesting story about a species of crustacean called the samurai crab, which is found in Japanese waters. This crab wears a pattern on its shell that resembles the face of a samurai warrior. It is thought by many that the honored face may be the result of *artificial*

selection. The theory contends that, over many years, Japanese fisherman were reluctant to eat such crabs and would release them back into the wild. The more samurai-looking the face, the greater the likelihood that the crab would be released. Thus, Japanese fisherman "selected" the best samurai crabs for survival. Though intriguing and seemingly logical, some scientists argue that the theory lacks critical biological evidence. True or not, it makes for a great story!

ABOVE:
Depiction of the Ghost of Taira Tomomori, Featuring Samurai Crabs with Faces of Fallen Soldiers. Utagawa Kuniyoshi, c. 1830. The

Heikea japonica, found in the waters off Japan, sports a shell with the face of a grimacing samurai warrior. Is this a case of artificial selection?

MIRAGES

Mirages are caused by light rays bending in response to differences in atmospheric temperature. Earth's atmosphere is like a many-layered cake. Each layer has a different temperature and density, and the boundaries between layers are where mirages appear. Such atmospheric boundaries sometimes act like shimmering mirrors, reflecting the sky or an object in the distance.

When the temperature above our line of sight is warmer than the temperature below it, we can sometimes see mirages of things that are beyond the horizon. There is a popular story from 1906 in which polar explorer Robert E. Peary witnessed a mirage while exploring Antarctica. Perry was convinced that he had discovered a new continent, but it was actually a *superior mirage* of a distant landmass located beyond the horizon. Peary named the new continent "Crocker Land" after one of his financial supporters and later sought additional funding to explore and settle the new territory. Oops.

ABOVE:

Sunset behind Atmospheric Layers. Two distinct atmospheric layers are evident in this superior mirage of a sunset. From this viewpoint, we can see two images of the setting sun. One is the actual sun; the other is a mirage.

Desert mirages are seen frequently because arid desert terrains are characterized by very hot surface temperatures that contrast with the dense, cooler air above. A mirage at ground level often occurs when a dense, cool layer of air, pressed down by heavier layers above, contrasts significantly with the ground temperature. In this case, an atmospheric mirror forms at ground level, refracting light rays from above and generating an *inferior mirage*. If you are on a low rise, you may see a shimmering blue lake in the middle of nowhere. The lake is merely a reflected image of the sky. A similar mirage is often visible when we drive through the desert on a hot day. The highway ahead may seem to shimmer like a glassy pool of water, as short stretches of the road plunge in and out of the plane of an atmospheric mirror.

BELOW:
A Desert Mirage. Travelers in this Egyptian desert will be disappointed to discover that the pool of water ahead is actually an inferior mirage.

BEDROCK BEAUTIES

Mother Nature provides a rich palette of terrain features that inspire the imagination. Explorers and settlers have found many familiar shapes as they moved across the country. Here are some of my favorite landscape feature illusions.

RIGHT:
Pictograph Cave State Park, Montana.

OPPOSITE, TOP:
Eagle Rock. As seen from Eagle Point on the west rim of the Grand Canyon, this formation resembles a soaring eagle.

OPPOSITE, BOTTOM:
Shiprock, in the Navajo Indian Nation, New Mexico.

8

FINGERTIP ILLUSIONS

But what has it got in his pocketses, eh?
Not string, precious, but not nothing.

—J.R.R. TOLKIEN, *THE HOBBIT*

Many of the illusions in this book can be used easily for group demonstrations. However, there are some excellent illusions specially designed for this purpose. These are some of my favorite "fingertip" illusions that you can carry around with you wherever you go. These little exercises don't require folding props, lights, or images, and you can demonstrate them with nothing up your sleeves but dirty elbows.

THE MYSTERY OF ARISTOTLE'S NOSE

It seems that apart from writing extensively about ethics, government, the scientific method, mathematics, logic, and poetry, Greek philosopher Aristotle also found time to fiddle with his nose. The only items you will need for this exercise are one nose and two fingertips.

To begin, relax and close your eyes. Now run your index and middle fingers gently up and down the bridge of your nose—both sides. The idea is to establish what your nose feels like. Keep a straight face, and try not to scratch *le nez!* Now, cross your fingers, close your eyes again, and run your fingertips down the length of your nose using both fingertips in the crossed position. *Yikes!* It will feel strange, as if you were touching someone else's nose.

OPPOSITE:
Statue of the ancient Greek philosopher Aristotle, located in his birthplace of Stagira, Halkidiki, Greece.

NEAR RIGHT:
Cross Your Fingers!

FAR RIGHT:
*Feeling the Nose with
Crossed Fingers.*
R. Ausbourne, 2009.
Model: Carmen Chavez.

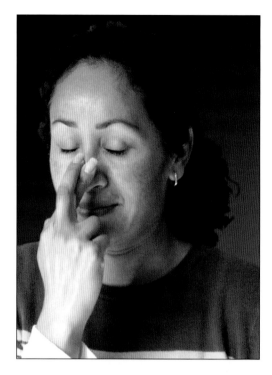

HOW IT WORKS

In the first demonstration, your schnoz feels normal because the brain received a message from each fingertip from where they should be—next to each other, with the index fingertip nearest the thumb and the middle fingertip nearest the ring finger. In the second demonstration, however, the brain receives the same messages but assumes that they came from the wrong fingers. The fingertips are not where they should be—they have switched places, but the brain hasn't caught on yet.

We can only imagine a scene with Aristotle stroking his own poetic proboscis with two fingers and a straight face. In any case, the illusory sensation wouldn't last forever if your fingers were crossed permanently. At some point your brain would catch on, and the illusion would fade.

THE FINGER SAUSAGE ILLUSION

This demonstration may look like a luncheon special, but it's actually an optical illusion that appears in the form of a cyclopean (one-eye) image. The only equipment you will need for this demonstration are your eyes and both index fingers. First, pick out an object to focus on—one farther away than your arms can comfortably reach. Look toward your target, reach out, and point your index fingers at each other in front of the target. A wall clock is used as an example in the figure below. Your fingertips should be lined up but not touching. Now, shift your focus beyond your fingertips to the target, but remain aware of your fingertips in the foreground. You will find them a bit fuzzy but very visible. Continue to focus beyond them and adjust your fingers until you see an illusion similar to the image shown in the example.

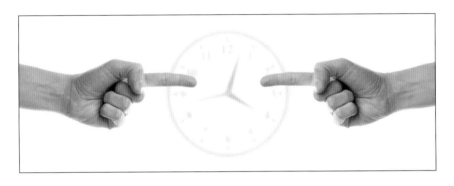

HOW IT WORKS

While you focus on your fingers, your eyes don't actually point straight ahead, but slightly inward. Thus, your lines of sight converge in a cone shape on your fingers. When you focus to the object beyond, the lines of sight become nearly parallel as you expand your view outward. Your fingers now occupy a different position relative to your lines of sight, appearing to overlap with each other. However, rather than merging the binocular images—one from each eye—into one cyclopean image, the brain forces the images to compete with each other. In one eye, the finger continues, while in the other, it ends and is replaced by the background. Because the latter image includes a high-contrast step from finger to background, it wins the battle, and the other image is suppressed. The resulting double image includes two high-contrast images of the gap between the two fingertips.

TWO-FINGERS ILLUSION

This illusion will produce an extra finger, visually speaking, should you ever need one. The simple demonstration requires only one finger and normal, binocular vision. Begin by focusing on a spot on a nearby wall. Hold up a finger between you and the wall. When you focus on your finger, you see only one, but when you focus on the wall beyond, you see two fingers.

HOW IT WORKS

When you focus on your finger, your eyes point inward very sharply, creating a very small angle of view. As you focus beyond your finger, the viewing angle increases. Your finger now occupies two positions relative to your lines of sight, so the brain generates a double image—two fingers, one for each eye.

OPPOSITE:
Two-Fingers Illusion.
R. Ausbourne, 2009.

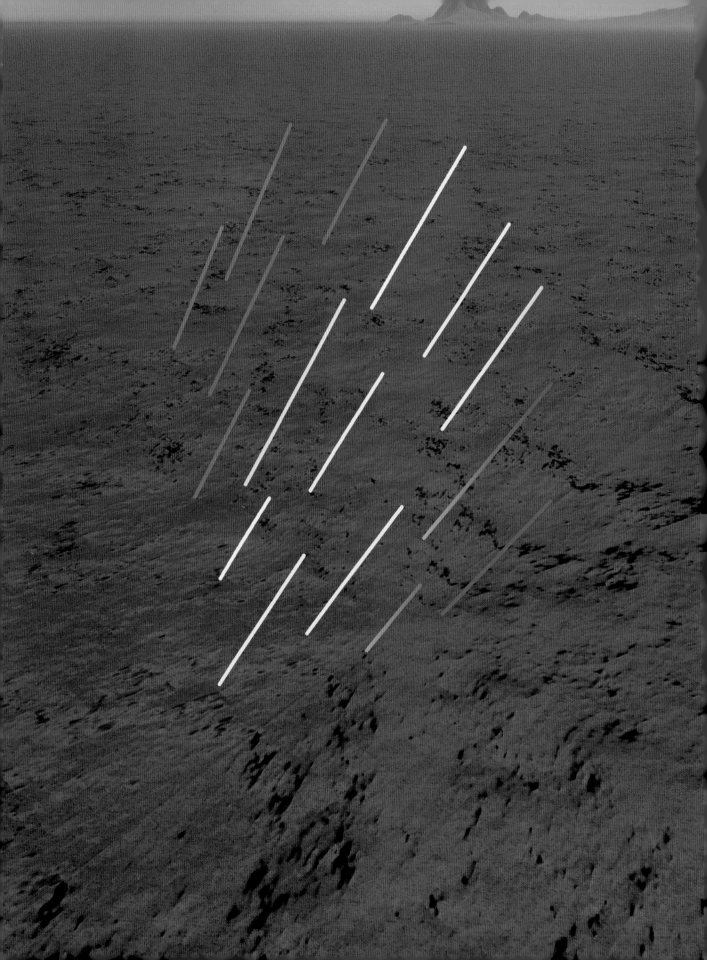

HIDDEN IN PLAIN SIGHT

Everything in Nature contains all the powers of Nature.
Everything is made of hidden stuff.

—RALPH WALDO EMERSON

The term *anamorphic,* when used in the context of illusions, refers to an image that contains an optically distorted puzzle. The images on page 137 are a popular type of anamorphic puzzle. A message has been optically distorted by stretching the letters to the extreme, so it looks more like a bar code than a sentence. To see the message, tilt the book back until it is almost flat and examine the inclusion from the bottom of the page. At this angle, the letters appear to have shrunk to normal height.

The above solution works with a certain type of anamorphic illusion, but not all of them. Sometimes a hidden aspect or message might be revealed; at other times the entire picture may change into something else. For anamorphic illusions, part of the fun is discovering how to look at the images in order to reveal the hidden message or object. Often, it's a matter of rotating, flipping, or tilting the drawing in a certain way, but some anamorphic illusions can be particularly devious.

OPPOSITE:
Red Planet. R. Ausbourne, 2008. Turn the page counterclockwise one-quarter turn and then tilt the book away from you until it is almost horizontal. If you examine the page from the bottom left-hand corner, the lines will stand up in 3-D.

LEFT:
Anamorphic View: Red Planet. R. Ausbourne, 2008.

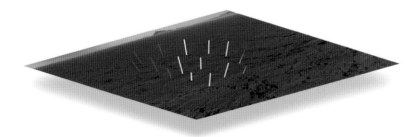

Inventor, artist, and weapons designer Leonardo da Vinci was famous for being concerned about espionage, so he often went to extremes to protect his ideas and notes. To avoid prying eyes, Leonardo took to composing his journal entries using a strange script—one could only read his notes by using a mirror. In fact, Leonardo da Vinci used anamorphic illusions to hide his secrets.

TOP:
Da Vinci Mirror Writing.
Sample of journal notes showing Leonardo's mirror-writing style.

RIGHT:
Da Vinci Self-Portrait.
Leonardo da Vinci,
c. 1510—1515.

OPPOSITE:
Trompe l'oeil Ceiling Fresco. Andrea Pozzo, c. 1690. This painted ceiling within the Church of Sant'Ignazio in Rome, is entirely flat, including the dome at the top of the photograph.

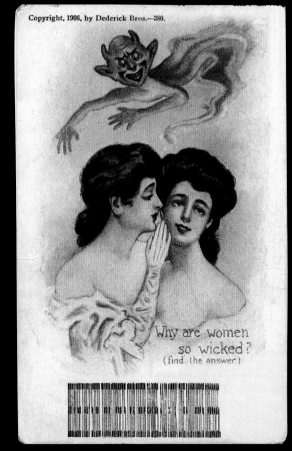

Copyright, 1906, by Dederick Bros.—380.

Why are women
so wicked?
(find the answer)

TOP:
*Vintage Postcard with
Anamorphic Message.*
R. Ausbourne, 2007. Tilt
the image and view the
heart from a low angle.
See page 150 for the
answer.

BOTTOM: *Why Are
Women So Wicked?*
Postcard,
c. 1906. Tilt the image
forward and view it
from below.
See page 150 for the
answer.

TOP:
An Anamorphic Revelation.
R. Ausbourne, 2008.
The message in this image is hidden in plain sight. If you stare at the image in the right way, it will reveal itself.
See page 150 for the answer.

BOTTOM:
Anamorphic Puzzle.
R. Ausbourne, 2009.
Tilt the image and view the picture along the plane of the page to reveal the solution. There is something special about the answer to this puzzle: It is also a palindrome (a word or sentence that reads the same way forward as it does backward).
See page 150 for the answer.

ABOVE:
Antique Mirror Anamorphosis. **Anonymous.** Here is an antique anamorphic print with the solution mirror shown in place.

The print is a copy of a popular painting from the beginning of the nineteenth century, when these puzzles were popular.

OPPOSITE, TOP :
Save the Whales. Anthony Azevedo, 1999. A diabolical form of anamorphic illusion in which a coherent image can only be seen by placing a mirrored tube in exactly the right spot.

OPPOSITE, BOTTOM :
Virtual Anamorphosis on Cylinder. Ruizo/Wikimedia, 2008. This is a handsome rendering of an anamorphic scene with a nonlinear mirror.

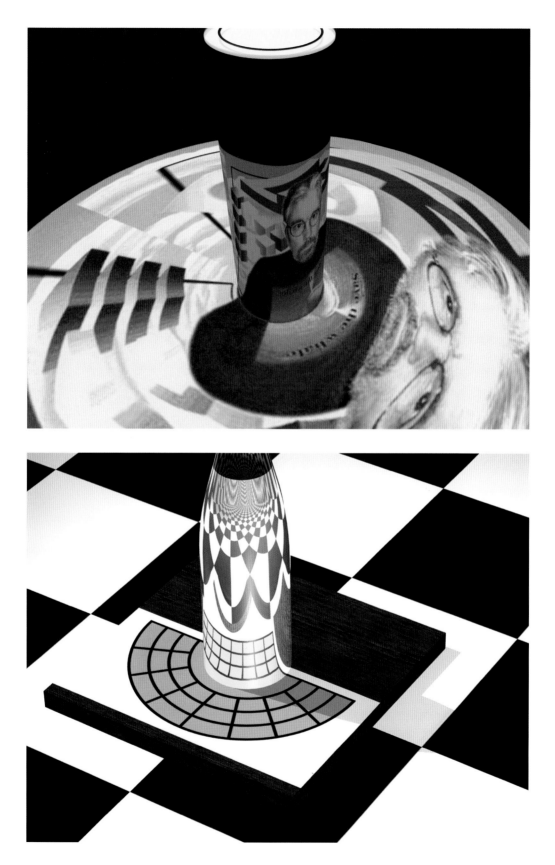

BILATERAL ILLUSIONS

Bilateral illusions are head-over-heels, topsy-turvy illusions. They are *ambiguous* because they have at least two aspects, and they are *anamorphic* because both aspects can only be seen by flipping them upside down. Thus, bilateral illusions may also be described as *anamorphic ambiguities*, a.k.a. *topsy-turvys*.

Here are some more of my favorite topsy-turvy illusions.

RIGHT:

The Vegetable Gardener. Giuseppe Arcimboldo, c. 1562. A student of Leonardo da Vinci, and later an imperial court painter, Arcimboldo pioneered the style of art we now call topsy-turvy.

OPPOSITE:

Japanese Reversibles. Anonymous. An ancient Japanese print showing a variety of unique topsy-turvys.

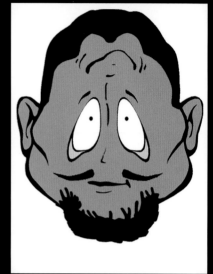

TOP LEFT:
Mon Oncle.
R. Ausbourne, 2009.
That's no uncle; that's
my mother-in-law in
her favorite hat.

TOP RIGHT:
Two Faces.
R. Ausbourne, 2009.
Cartoon faces often
come with another
face on the flip side.

BOTTOM LEFT:
The Cop and the Horse.
Anonymous. To help
this horse find its rider,
turn the picture
upside down.

BOTTOM RIGHT:
Happy & Sad.
Anonymous. This little
gem was printed on the
back of an eighteenth-
century pocket mirror.
Turn it upside down to
see the illusion.

British war posters often used topsy-turvy designs featuring the former British Secretary of State Lord Horatio Herbert Kitchener and former German emperor, Kaiser Wilhelm II.

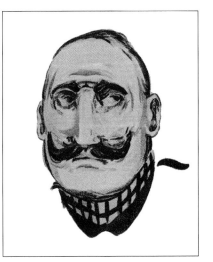

TOP LEFT:
World War I British Poster 1. The caption for this image reads, "The British Bulldog . . . puts the Germans on the run!"

TOP RIGHT:
World War I British Poster 2. This poster shows the Kaiser with a noose around his neck. The caption reads, "To find the person who put the rope around the Kaiser's neck . . . turn this picture upside down!"

BOTTOM LEFT:
World War I British Poster 3. This poster features a stern-looking Kaiser. The caption reads, "When German junkerism is completely overthrown, you will see Kitchener satisfied."

BOTTOM RIGHT:
World War I British Poster #4. In this poster, the Kaiser is looking around in a furtive manner. The caption reads, "The Kaiser and . . . Another reverse for him!"

STEREOSCOPIC ILLUSIONS

Many of us are familiar with a form of 3-D illusions called *stereograms,* in which one is asked to stare, trancelike, at a distorted image until multiple fields of random dots merge into a 3-D image. Unlike some popular illusions, stereoscopic illusions are stable and admirably three-dimensional. Also, the viewing technique required for this type of illusion is easy to master.

Stereoscopic illusions work because of our binocular vision. Each eye captures a separate image, which the brain then combines into one. You can see how this works by looking at an object (such as this page) and then alternately blinking your right eye, and then your left. The object will appear to shift back and forth slightly with each alternating blink. This shift in the position of the object is called a *parallax,* and the amount of shift is determined by the distance between your eyes as well as the distance between you and the object. When you open both eyes, the object appears in the center as a single 3-D stereo image. Stereoscopic illusions utilize pairs of printed images, one for each eye. The *Distorted Square and Jupiter* illusion is a typical stereoscopic illusion. The images are separated by a space almost equidistant to the space between your eyes. Also note that the images are not identical.

BELOW:
Distorted Square and Jupiter. R. Ausbourne, 2009. This is the *Distorted Square* illusion in 3-D, plus the planet Jupiter with three of her moons. Follow directions in the accompanying text to see the 3-D effect.

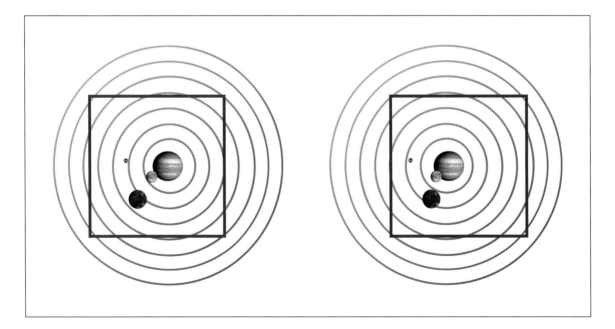

To master the viewing technique for the following illusions, focus on the center of each one, between the pair of images, from a comfortable reading distance. Now, gently begin to cross your eyes, as if you were trying to see a ladybug on your nose. If it helps, place an index finger on your nose and focus on it. As you cross your eyes, you will see the images merge to form a third image in the center. If you see four images, you've gone too far. After a few tries, you will find that you can easily stabilize the third image, which is in 3-D!

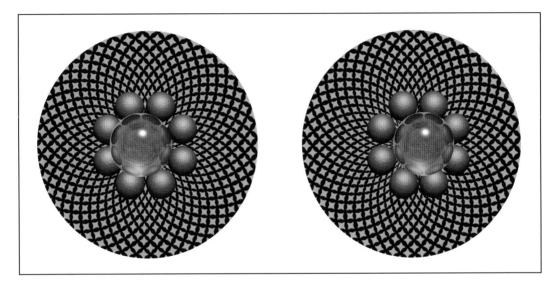

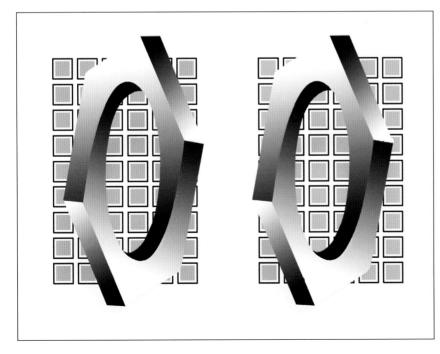

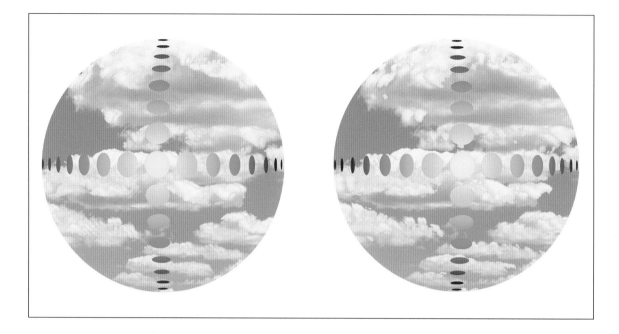

TOP:

Ovals over Clouds.
R. Ausbourne, 2009.
The dots do not appear
to converge in the exact
centers of each circle.
How will they project in
3-D? Follow directions
on page 145 to view.

BOTTOM:

*Flashing Design and
Cameo.* R. Ausbourne,
2009. Two different
illusions are combined
in this example. Follow
directions on page 145
to view the *Mystic Wheel*
and the *Woman of the
World* illusions in 3-D.

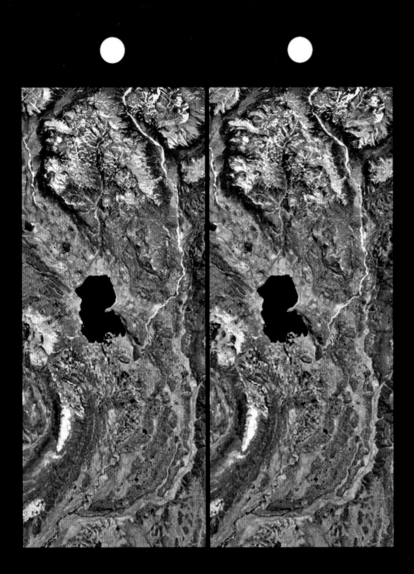

ABOVE:
3-D View of Lake Palanskoye, Russia.
These are actual photos of Lake Palanskoye in Russia, taken from orbit. Stare at the photos and cross your eyes slightly until a third white dot appears between the two. The new, center image is 3-D!

ACKNOWLEDGMENTS

Many thanks go to Vivian and Ken Nagy for their constant support. Thanks to Charles H. Brittenham Jr.: honcho, friend, mentor, and source of exuberant inspiration. Thanks to the artists, photographers, and a myriad of *illusionistas* who have graciously contributed their work to the whole, with a special thanks to Josh Sommers. Profound gratitude to every scientist who has ever drawn a breath. And, finally, thanks to Betty Loraine Ausbourne—cook, baker, bicycle fixer, landscape engineer, and mentor—for believing in me, always. *Thanks, Mom!*

ABOVE:
Tiger Face. Chuck Brittenham, 2007.

PUZZLE ANSWERS

CHAPTER 3

CHAPTER 6

Mystery Dot Quiz (page 103): Pink

Afterimage Field Test (page 106): For each pair of color dots on the left, you should see an imaginary pair of dots in opposite colors within the targets on the right. The opposite colors you should see are approximately: (1) yellow-pink, (2) violet-pink, (3) orange-blue, (4) white-white, (5), yellow-white.

I Have a Dream (page 107): Dr. Martin Luther King Jr.

Italian Navigator (page 107): Christopher Columbus.

Good-bye Norma Jean (page 107): Marilyn Monroe.

Historical Figures 1 (page 108): Ulysses S. Grant, Abraham Lincoln, Che Guevara.

Historical Figures 2 (page 109): Hopalong Cassidy, Charles Lindbergh, Jesus of Nazareth.

Historical Figures 3 (page 110): Greta Garbo, the *Mona Lisa,* President Barack Obama.

Historical Figures 4 (page 111): George Washington, Theodore Roosevelt, Queen Victoria.

CHAPTER 9

Vintage Postcard with Anamorphic Message (page 136): Love me Little Love me Long.

Why Are Women So Wicked? (page 136): Because they steel their corsets, crib their babies, and hook one another's dresses.

An Anamorphic Revelation (page 137): You Won't Believe Your Eyes!

Anamorphic Puzzle (page 137): Are we not drawn onward, we few, drawn onward to new era?

NOTES

CHAPTER 1

1. A. Hurlbert, "Colour Vision: Primary Visual Cortex Shows Its Influence," *Current Biology* 13 (2003): 270–272.

2. Vilayanur S. Ramachandran and Diane Rogers-Ramachandran, "Mind the Gap," *Scientific American Reports: Special Edition on Perception* (2008): 4–7.

3. Vilayanur S. Ramachandran and Diane Rogers-Ramachandran, "The Reality of Illusory Contours," *Scientific American Reports: Special Edition on Perception* (2008): 42–43.

CHAPTER 2

1. Vilayanur S. Ramachandran and Diane Rogers-Ramachandran, "Ambiguities and Perception," *Scientific American Reader to Accompany Schacter/Gilbert/Wegner,* ed. Daniel L. Schacter (New York: Macmillan, 2008), 56–59. Ramachandran and Rogers-Ramachandran are affiliated with the Center for Brain and Cognition at the University of California, San Diego.

CHAPTER 3

1. Mark Changizi, *The Vision Revolution* (Dallas: BenBella Books, 2010).

2. John S. Werner, Baingio Pinna, et al., "Illusory Color and the Brain," *Scientific American Reports: Special Edition on Perception* (2008): 90–95.

3. Illustration adapted from *Treasure Island* by Robert Louis Stevenson (New York: Scribner's, 1911, illustrated by N. C. Wyeth).

4. Werner, Pinna, et al., "Illusory Color and the Brain."

BIBLIOGRAPHY

Ausbourne, Robert. *How to Understand, Enjoy and Draw Optical Illusions.* San Francisco: Pomegranate, 2007.

Block, J. R. *Seeing Double.* New York: Routledge, 2002.

Changizi, Mark. *The Vision Revolution*, Dallas, TX: BenBella Books, 2009.

Langdon, John. *Wordplay.* New York: Harcourt Brace Jovanovich, 1992.

Ord, Colin. *Magic Moving Images.* St. Albans: Tarquin, 2007.

Wick, Walter. *Walter Wick's Optical Tricks.* New York: Scholastic, 2008.

INTERNET RESOURCES

"Adding Depth to Illusions," Lock Haven University, http://www.lhup.edu/~dsimanek/3d/illus2.htm

"Akiyoshi's illusion pages," Department of Psychology, Ritsumeikan University, http://www.ritsumei.ac.jp/~akitaoka/index-e.html

"Chinese-English Bilingual Ambigrams," http://www.cognitive-china.org/

"Einstein Ring in Distant Universe," European Southern Obervatory, http://www.eso.org/public/news/eso0521/

Institute of Learning and Brain Sciences, University of Washington, http://ilabs.washington.edu/

"Key to All Optical Illusions Discovered," LiveScience.com, http://www.livescience.com/4950-key-optical-illusions-discovered.html

Mighty Optical Illusions, http://www.moillusions.com/

"Motion Induced Blindness," on Michael Bach's 92 Visual Phenomena & Optical Illusions, http://www.michaelbach.de/ot/mot_mib/index.html

Optische Taeuschungen, http://www.cg.tuwien.ac.at/courses/Seminar/WS2005/index.php/Optische_Taeuschungen#Afterimages

SandlotScience.com, http://www.sandlotscience.com/

PHOTO CREDITS

GENERAL INDEX

INDEX OF ILLUSTRATIONS